The
Spice of Life
Cookbook

The Spice of Life Cookbook

DAVID WADE

WORD BOOKS, PUBLISHER
Waco, Texas

THE SPICE OF LIFE COOKBOOK

Library of Congress catalog card number: 74–27480
Printed in the United States of America

To four of the
loveliest Christian
ladies I know

my sisters—
Mabel Wade Nicholson
Lorene Wade Blanton
Doris Wade Varley
Gena Wade Townley

They have loved
inspired and
supported me since
I was a small child.

Table of Contents

Preface

We are what we think and what we eat. From the beginning of time, man's purpose and his sustenance have been so closely linked that God's journal, the Holy Bible, reports in parallel this association.

Adam and Eve broke the Lord's law and partook of one of the forbidden fruits. This changed forever the course of mankind.

Man did eat angels' food: he sent them meat to the full.

Ps. 78:25

While in Egypt, the Israelites savored many vegetables including cucumbers, leeks, onions, garlic, beans, and lentils. Wild game was the principle source of meat supply. Quail, pigeons, fowl, turtledoves, and eggs from wild birds embraced their diet. Once these people migrated from Egypt to the Sinai Desert, they were forty years without such delicacies. Only God's bread of heaven, better known as manna, sustained them. Manna, an excretion of two scale insects living on the twigs of the tamarisk bush, was provided by God to keep the Israelites alive. Every morning this fine flakelike product was found on the ground. It resembled hoarfrost. It had the taste of coriander seed, was white, but its sweet honey wafer flavor was pleasing. Manna can still be found today near the Sinai Mountains.

The Bible clearly chronicles the importance of food in the lives of the Hebrews and early Christians. Crop failure, famine, and the lack of a good trade system were constant threats to their livelihood. The simple harvest, storage, and preparation of food was a significant part of man's life. During sacrificial ceremonies and the celebration of other religious occasions, livestock was slaugh-

9

tered, but for the most part animals that produced milk for curd and cheese were hardly ever used for food.

The basic techniques of cooking during biblical days were simply roasting and boiling. The addition of herbs and spices added flavor to their recipes. Figs and grapes were the primary source of sweets with grain and barley being ground for flour. A variety of breads and cakes were developed from this flour. Cereal, too, was common food fare and early Christians expanded their compendium of taste-mosphere to include all kinds of fish, chicken, and hen eggs. Olives and olive oil were of paramount importance to the kitchens in these early times.

Joel discussed apple trees that were destroyed by locusts and Solomon described the same fruit as most refreshing.

Every covenant and contract during early biblical days was celebrated with a repast. To refuse an invitation to dine was a symbol of broken fellowship. From Genesis to Revelation, biblical man regarded his food as a divine gift from God.

Our generous supply and great variety of foods today are still divine gifts from our Heavenly Father. What we think and what we eat are still the basis of our existence, and this publication I hope will call attention to the association of faith and food.

Good living and bon appétit.

David Wade

And also that every man should eat and drink, and enjoy the good of all his labour, it is the gift of God.

Ecclesiastes 3:13

Menus

AFTER-THE-GAME BUFFET

Vegetable-Relish Kabobs (31)
Festive Macaroni Salad (62)
Fillet Burgers, Gourmet (72)
Toasted Buns
Baked Beans in Chafing Dish (128)
or Deviled Eggs in Creole Sauce (95)
Broiled Tomatoes Parmesan (161)
or Peach Catsup Garnish (35)
Boston Brown Bread (182) with Cream Cheese Spread
Iced Tea, with Spice (222)
Grapefruit Pie (189)

AFTER-THE-MUSICAL DINNER

After-Five Canapés (29)
Manhattan Clam Chowder (109)
Asparagus Spears with Tomato Slices (53)
Cauliflowerets with Capers (138)
The New French Dressing (53)
Steak Bordelaise (67)
Spaghetti with Sauce Italia (79)
(Swiss Noodles) (173)
Eggplant Au Gratin, Stuffed (144)
(Empire State Red Beans) (127)
Rye Loaf Bread   Coffee
Peach Melba (202)
After-Dinner Candies

15

AFTER-THE-PLAY OLD SOUTH DINNER

Gourmet Salad with French Dressing (58)
Spiced Peaches
Sweet and Sour Pork Chops (83)
(Candied Sweet Potatoes) (83)
Green Beans Carolina (122) or Scalloped Turnips (163)
Macaroni Cheese Bake (172) or Hopping John (150)
Onion Shortbread (181)   Coffee
Charlotte Russe Economy (202)

A POLYNESIAN TABLE

Iced Cherry-Tomato Gelatin Salad (60)
Egg and Endive Garnish—Mayonnaise
Shrimp with Peppers (113)
Vegetable-Cheese Bake (168) or Island Cabbage (135)
Luau Corn (142) or Celery Oriental (140)
Grape Hawaiian Punch (221)
French Bread Loaf (179)
Fruit-Coconut Dessert
in Melon Halves (198)

16

BEACHCOMBER DINNER

Coconut Soup Polynesian (43)
Carrot Salad Hawaiian (55)
Bar Harbor Fish Platter (113)
Sautéed Onion Slices (147)
Cheese Log (171)
Gulfstream Shrimp Snacks (31)
Cabbage and Brussels Sprouts Oriental (134)
Beachboy Beans Baked in Tomatoes (126)
Pretzels, Crackers   The Menehune (223)
Miami Beach Lime Chiffon Dessert (206)

CHILDREN'S PATRIOTIC PARTY DINNER

Buttered Popcorn
Fruit Cocktail Orange Jello (207)
Corny Dog Centerpiece (93)
Stuffed Eggs (35)   Bacon Slices
Apple Juice (227)
Corn on the Cob (141)   Paper Cup French Fries (151)
Gingerbread Cut-Outs (192)
Chocolate and White
Combination Cake (190)

17

EAST INDIAN DINNER

Lotus Salad and Eastern Yogurt Dip (57)
Tomato Chutney (36)
Lamb Jerusalem (89)
Rice and Apples (89)
Sabzi (166)
Tuna with Curry Sauce Intrigue (117)
Orange-Cashew Rice Bowl (156)
Assorted Fruits
Broiled-Skewered Lamb Cubes (90)
Indo-Spices   Indo-Condiments   Indo-Side Dishes
(89, 157)
Bananas Mediterranean (197)
Hot Tea

EUROPEAN DINNER

Iced Asparagus Soup (41)
Cauliflower Salad with Lisbon Dressing (56)
Fricassee of Liver Françoise (95)
Spinach Europa (159) or Celery Madrid (140)
Honey-Almond Sweet Potato Whip (154)
or Red Cabbage Dover (136)
Swiss Strawberry Cheese Cake (195)
Croissants   Coffee

18

FAMILY WEDNESDAY NIGHT DINNER

Quick and Savory Tomato Soup with Croutons (43)
Assorted Cheeses and Grapes
Southern Beef Loaf (74)
Pimiento Cheese Corn Cups (144) or Angel Corn (141)
Onions Wisconsin (149)
or Imperial Brussels Sprouts (133)
Iced Tea   Heat-and-Serve Rolls
Pineapple Upside-Down Cake (192)

GUADALAJARA MEXICAN DINNER

Guacamole Salad (51)
Green Peppers, Red Peppers, Green Onions, and Olives
Texas Chili Con Carne (81)
Spanish Rice (157) or Hominy Cheese Ring (146)
Sautéed Squash and Onions (160)
or Scalloped Tomatoes (162)
Bean Tacos (94)
Tortillas   Coffee
Orange-Nut Frozen Sundae (200)

INTIMATE DINNER FOR TWO

Raspberry Cheese Bouquet Salad (50)
Chicken Tetrazzini (104)
Baked Zucchini with Cheese in Shells (161)
or Celery Au Gratin (139)
Green Beans and Onions, Tempura (123)
or Indian Cabbage (136)
Iced Tea   Peppered Bread, Grilled (179)
Pots de Crème (204)

ITALIAN OPERA DINNER

Antipasto Tray (30)   Shrimp Cocktail (32)
Italian Spaghetti with Meat Sauce (78)
(Parmesan Cheese)
Cauliflower with Cheese Sauce (138)
or Italian Eggplant (145)
Italian Salad (59) or Garden Pasta (163)
Italian Pizza (Bacon and Cheese) (90)
Coffee
Italian Custard (204)

20

KING-OF-THE-BARBECUE STEAK DINNER

Salad Tray with
Lettuce Quarters,
Sliced Tomatoes, Avocado Dip,
and Corn Chips (52)
Steak Durango (67)
Whipped Potatoes and Brown Gravy (153)
Barbecued Wax Beans (129) or Onions and Bacon (148)
Terero Corn (143) or Ranchers' Beans (126)
Hot Mocha Drink (215)   Bread
Doughnut Cake (191)

LADIES' LUNCHEON

Relish Bowl of Cream Cheese
Balls, Radishes, Olives
Chilled Cream of Avocado Soup (41)
Miami Fruit Salad Platter with Citrus Dressing (48)
Chicken Imperial (100)
Savory New Potatoes and Carrots with Chives (166)
or Butter-Meg Potatoes (151)
Cream of the Crop Baby Lima Casserole (125)
or Asparagus Parmesan (121)
Pecan-Corn Muffins Petite (181)   Iced Tea
Apricot Meringue Torte (196)

21

NEW ENGLAND SUNDAY DINNER

Hot Applesauce Compote (207)
Cottage Cheese-Cranberry Salad (50)
Leg of Lamb (87)
Connecticut Bread-Nut Stuffing (183)
Boiled Onions and Carrots (88)
Gravy of Lamb (88)
Down East Potatoes in Ceramic Shells (154)
or Tomatoes 'n' Rice (155)
Yankee Doodle Bean Ring (123)
or Green Bean Pickles, Vermont (36)
Hot Tea with Cinnamon Sticks and Whole Cloves
English Muffins with Grape Jelly, Orange Marmalade,
Black Raspberry Jam
Peach Waffle Shortcake, Boston (201)

NEW ORLEANS CREOLE DINNER
(For when the boss comes)

Layered Salad in Glass
with Bleu Cheese Dressing (59–60)
Jambalaya (110)
Broccoli New Orleans (132)   Plantation Okra (147)
Fresh Peach Broil (201)
Celery-French Green Bean Medley (122)
Fritter Corn Bread (180)
Hot Peppers
Louisiana Coffee Creole (215)
Crepes d'Orange (199)
French Quarter Pralines (205)

22

NOCTURNAL SUPPER

Emerald Mound Salad (47)
Holiday Fruit Soup (42)
Swedish Meat Balls (77)
Cashew Green Beans (124) or Holiday Cabbage (134)
Tomato-Cheese Scandia (162) or Squash Loaf (160)
Coffee   Parker House Rolls
Pound Cake with
Lemon-Coconut Icing (193)

OLD-FASHIONED DINNER FOR
GRANDMOTHER AND GRANDFATHER

Hot Potato Salad (62)
Beets and Onions, Harvard style (131)
Roast Chicken (103)
Buttered Spinach (158) Baked Acorn Squash (159)
Sweet Carrot Bake (137) or Creamed Limas (124)
Homemade Bread Loaves (177)
Coffee and Milk
Miniature Apple Dumplings (187)

23

SMORGASBORD

Arctic Fruit Salad (49)
Salmon Salad (64)
Trout in Sour Cream Mayonnaise (116)
Ham Scandinavian (85)
Meat Balls Finlandia (75)
Broiled Grapefruit Northern (199)
Lazy Susan of Vegetables (164)
Smorgasbord Relishes (37)
White Bread Loaf, Scandia (178)
Date-Nut Bread (182)
Coffee
Spice Cake (194)
Cherry Meringues (197)

SPORTSMEN'S BANQUET

Spicy Red and White Slaw (55)
Derby Cheese Assortment (172)
Sandwich Tray (29)
Sportsmen's Stew (70)
Wieners-Tomatoes-Onions on Hibachi (92)
*Rainbow Trout with Noodles, Buttered and
Breaded (115)*
Baked Sweet Potatoes (155)
Pork and Beans in Peppers (128)
Hard-Cooked Eggs and Green Onions
Hunter's Punch (230)
Coffee
Cherry Cobbler Jubilee (188)

24

SUMMERTIME BACKYARD DINNER

Corn Relish Salad (56)
Garden Fresh Kabobs (30)
Pickle Scramble (37)
Sweet-and-Sour Spare Ribs (84)
Patio Pizza (91) or Cheese Balls (171)
Green Peas and Green Limas, Roma (167)
or Herbed Brussels Sprouts (133)
Texas Cooler (226)
Apple Cream Pie (188)

WEDDING REHEARSAL SUPPER

Waldorf Salad Gourmet (51)
Chicken Salad (with Cucumber Slices) (63)
Rice Supreme (156)
Asparagus Royal (121) or Broccoli-Hollandaise (132)
Creamy Peas in Patty Shells (150)
or Braised Celery and Tomatoes (139)
Apple Juice (227)
Coffee
Crackers
Bread
Ice Cream Sundae Pie (203)

WESTERN DINNER

Ranch Bean Salad (61)
Spicy Tomato-Cucumber Soup (44)
Broiled Ham Slices with Apple and Pineapple Rings (87)
Cream of Hominy Casserole (146)
or Corn Pudding (142)
Vegetable Trio Brussels Sprouts-Squash-Okra (164)
or Chili Stuffed Onions (148)
Iced Tea
Corn Muffins (180)
Texas Pecan Pie (190)

WHEN THE PREACHER COMES FOR SUNDAY DINNER

Cucumber-Tomato Slaw with Vinegar Dressing (54)
Round Roast (68) with Peach-Raspberry Garnish (69)
Baked Russets with Cheese and Bacon (152)
French Style Peas (149) or Spicy Green Beans (124)
Fresh Buttered Carrots (137) or Shredded Beets (131)
Coffee   Milk
French Bread Loaf with Parsley Butter (179)
Strawberry Long Cake (194)

26

Appetizers

Once I was piloting an airplane with my son, Doug, and niece, Joyce, as passengers. The craft began to mush and was about to stall on take-off. I suddenly realized that I was flying downwind. . . . "And if we know that he hear us, whatsoever we ask, we know that we have the petitions that we desired of him" (1 John 5:15) . . . flashed through my mind and I prayed the speediest prayer in history. At that moment, a great buoyancy seemed to lift the plane skyward. At a safe altitude, I looked back at the airport and the wind-tee was still indicating downwind. Since that experience, I have always believed in prayer.

AFTER-FIVE CANAPÉS

Many flavors of canapés may be made using cream cheese as a binder. Choose from the following ingredients for a variety of good canapés. Make any combination you think may delight the taste of your family and friends.

Cream cheese for as many
   canapés as desired
Mayonnaise
Pimiento
Pickle relish
Prepared mustard
Tiny cocktail onions
Capers
Snipped parsley
Love

Salt
Pepper
Paprika
Garlic salt
Seasoned salt
Worcestershire powder
Other spicy seasonings
Crackers (each box dif-
   ferent) suitable for can-
   apé construction
Patience

Some good combinations for canapés are: cream cheese mixed with mayonnaise and pimiento; cream cheese and pickle relish; cream cheese with mustard, mayonnaise, and tiny cocktail onions. Some are topped with capers and others sprinkled with parsley. All are seasoned with salt, pepper, and paprika. Garlic salt, seasoned salt, Worcestershire powder, and other spicy seasonings are available for canapés.

A small boy was asked if his family prayed before meals. He replied no, because his mother is a good cook.

SANDWICH TRAY

29

Alternate slices of sandwich bread, ham, bologna, Swiss cheese, and American cheese slices. Garnish with pickles and radishes.

ANTIPASTO TRAY

This is an Italian relish dish which is easy to prepare. All of the ingredients may be prepared as they are placed on the tray.

OUR ANTIPASTO TRAY INCLUDES:

Olives, green and ripe ones   Sliced tomatoes
Triangles of salami   Carrot sticks
Triangles of Italian cheese   Crabapples
Celery sticks   Patience
Love

OTHER CHOICES FOR THE ANTIPASTO MIGHT BE:

Pepperoni slices   Pickled cauliflower
Anchovies   Peppers, sweet, red, or
Artichoke hearts   green, sliced

Arrange the various foods on a tray or large platter in an attractive pattern and serve before the main dishes.

My doctrine shall drop as the rain, my speech shall distil as the dew, as the small rain upon the tender herb, and as the showers upon the grass. Deut. 32:2

30

GARDEN FRESH KABOBS

1 head cabbage   Mushrooms
Radishes   Pickles
Green peppers   Squash
Love   Patience

Use the cabbage head as a base. On small skewers alternate radishes, green pepper pieces, mushrooms, pickles, and squash pieces. To serve, punch skewers into cabbage head.

VEGETABLE-RELISH KABOBS

Small new potatoes, peeled
  and cooked
Small onions, skinned
Green pepper, sliced end
  pieces
Large dill pickles, sliced in
  large pieces
Green olives, without pits

Hot peppers
Radishes
Large button mushrooms
Oil
Apple cider vinegar
Salt
Love
Patience

Thread vegetables and relishes in alternating patterns for variety and color combinations on cocktail skewers. Dip each threaded kabob into mixture of half oil and half vinegar. Place kabobs on paper towels to drain off excess oil. Salt potatoes and arrange kabobs on a serving platter.

GULFSTREAM SHRIMP SNACKS

2 lbs. shelled and deveined
  frozen shrimp
3 bay leaves
1 tablespoon whole all-
  spice
1½ teaspoons crushed red
  pepper
2 teaspoons whole black
  pepper
2 teaspoons whole cloves
2 quarts water

2 medium-sized onions,
  sliced
6 cloves garlic
2 lemons, sliced
¼ cup salt
Toothpicks
2 Gouda cheese balls
Extra lemon slices for
  garnish
Love
Patience

31

Tie spices in a piece of cheesecloth. To water add onion, garlic, 2 sliced lemons, salt, and cheesecloth bag of seasonings and bring to a boil. Add frozen shrimp. Cover and return to the boiling point. Simmer 3 to 5 minutes, depending on size of shrimp. Remove pan from heat and let shrimp stand in spiced water for 3 minutes. Drain and chill. Insert one end of toothpick in shrimp and other end into Gouda cheese balls. Garnish with lemon slices.

SHRIMP COCKTAIL

1 lb. shelled and deveined frozen shrimp	Cocktail Sauce
	Lemon slices
½ head of shredded lettuce	Love
	Patience

Cook shrimp according to directions on package. Drain and chill. Arrange shredded lettuce in sherbet glasses filling them about ⅔ full. Allow about 8 to 10 shrimp per serving. Place shrimp atop lettuce with shrimp tails up and over the sides of sherbet glasses. In the middle place a generous amount of Cocktail Sauce. Provide lemon slices on the side dish.

COCKTAIL SAUCE:

1 cup catsup	1 teaspoon Worcestershire powder
2 tablespoons vinegar	
1 tablespoon horseradish	Dash of Tabasco
1 tablespoon minced celery	½ teaspoon salt

Blend together all ingredients. Chill in refrigerator. Makes 1¼ cups.

Relishes

Strength and honour are her clothing; and she shall rejoice in time to come. She openeth her mouth with wisdom; and in her tongue is the law of kindness. She looketh well to the ways of her household, and eateth not the bread of idleness. Her children arise up, and call her blessed; her husband also, and he praiseth her. Many daughters have done virtuously, but thou excellest them all.

Prov. 31:25–29

A movie star once said to me, "David, beauty is skin deep, but ugly goes all the way to the bone."

To me, the most beautiful person in the world is a Lady on the street, a Woman in the home, and a Mother on her knees.

PEACH CATSUP GARNISH

6 or 8 canned cling peach halves
2 tablespoons melted butter

1 tablespoon catsup for each peach half
Love
Patience

Arrange peaches on broiler, cut side up, and brush with melted butter. Spread top of each peach with catsup. Place about 3 inches from the heat and broil about 10 minutes or until peaches are heated through and topping bubbles up slightly. 6 servings.

He becometh poor that dealeth with a slack hand: but the hand of the diligent maketh rich.
Prov. 10:4

Success is an idea dressed in work clothes.

STUFFED EGGS

12 hard-boiled eggs (will make 24 halves for serving)
Mayonnaise
Dash of mustard
Love

Salt
Pepper
Little pickle relish (if your children like it)
Paprika
Patience

Cool and shell eggs; then cut in halves. Remove the yolks and mash well. Add mayonnaise, mustard, salt, pepper, pickle relish if desired, and mash together, blending well. Return egg yolk mixture to the egg white half-shells. Sprinkle with paprika and serve.

35

TOMATO CHUTNEY

1 tablespoon shortening	4 medium to large toma-
1 red chili pepper, minced	toes, peeled
½ teaspoon cumin seed	1 lemon, sliced
¼ teaspoon mustard seed	⅓ cup raisins
¼ teaspoon nutmeg	½ cup sugar
Love	Patience

Melt shortening in a skillet. Add red chili pepper, cumin seed, mustard seed, and nutmeg. When seeds begin to pop, add the peeled tomatoes which have been sliced ⅛ to ¼ inch thick. Place lemon slices on top. Simmer and stir often. Cook for 15 minutes. Add raisins and sugar. Keep simmering and stirring until mixture thickens, which will be about 30 minutes. Chill and serve.

If desired, you can pack the chutney in jars and seal for future use. Recipe makes about 1 pint.

It is easy to determine the involvement and activity of a person by the measure of his failures.

GREEN BEAN PICKLES, VERMONT

2 large cans (1 lb. each)	1½ cups vinegar
green beans, drained	½ teaspoon salt
3 Bermuda onions, sliced	2 cinnamon sticks
1 cup water	Dash Tabasco
1 cup brown sugar	Patience
Love	

36

Layer green beans and sliced onions in a bowl. Boil together for 3 minutes the remaining ingredients and pour over beans and onions. When cooled, store in the refrigerator. Let stand 24 hours before serving. This recipe will keep indefinitely.

PICKLE SCRAMBLE

1 bottle (1 lb.) whole dill
   pickles
1 bottle (1 lb.) whole sweet
   pickles

1 bottle (1 lb.) whole sour
   pickles
1 cup sugar
Love
Patience

Reserving juice from each jar, drain and slice all pickles into strips or quarter lengthwise. Combine juice from each jar and add sugar. Stir well. Mix pickles together and add to pickle liquid. Let stand in a large covered jar (or return mixed pickles to individual jars) for 12 hours or more. The longer their flavors mix together, the better and crisper the pickles. (For those who like pickles, this is a super pickle recipe.)

A young man asked his minister if he could live a good Christian life on his small salary of two hundred dollars a month. The minister replied, "That is all you can do."

SMORGASBORD RELISHES

Sauerkraut
Bread-and-butter pickles
Pickled green tomatoes
Sweet green relish
Sweet red pepper relish
Love

Anchovies
Lemon bits and snipped
   parsley for garnish of
   canapés
Crackers for canapés
Patience

37

Put sauerkraut in a crock. In individual matching trays place other relishes. To make anchovy canapés, put an anchovy in the center of each cracker and garnish with lemon bits and snipped parsley.

Soups

Then he answered and spake unto me, saying, This is the word of the Lord unto Zerubbabel, saying, Not by might, nor by power or might, nor are they lasting.

Zech. 4:6

Nothing worthwhile has ever been accomplished with great power or might nor is it lasting.

Spirit is the greatest force in the world: invisible like a great wind during an ocean storm but when properly directed, bringing about good results in any situation of life. Spirit is actually enthusiasm which is derived from the Greek word "en theō" meaning "in God."

CHILLED CREAM
OF AVOCADO SOUP

1½ cups mashed avocado
1 cup hot chicken stock
Cayenne
Black pepper
1½ cups heavy cream
½ cup sauterne cooking
    wine

1 teaspoon lemon juice
Salt
Parsley sprigs for garnish
4–6 tablespoons mayon-
    naise for garnish
Love
Patience

Stir mashed avocado into hot chicken stock and press the mixture through a fine sieve. Season avocado mixture with dash of cayenne and pepper to taste. Stir in the heavy cream, sauterne, and lemon juice. Season to taste with salt. Chill soup. Serve with sprigs of parsley and top each serving with a tablespoon of mayonnaise.

ICED ASPARAGUS SOUP

2 lbs. fresh asparagus
    (or 4 pkgs. frozen aspara-
    gus)
1 bunch scallions, thinly
    sliced
¼ cup flour
¼ cup water, generous

2 cups chicken stock
Salt
White pepper
1 cup heavy cream
Green pepper for garnish
Love
Patience

Cut the tips from asparagus and set them aside. Remove any tough white ends from stalks and discard. Slice the stalks in 2-inch pieces and put in a saucepan with the scallions and a generous ¼ cup water. Cover pan and cook very slowly until vegetables are tender. Add flour

Ho, every one that thirsteth, come ye to the waters, and he that hath no money; come ye, buy, and eat; yea, come, buy wine and milk without money and without price.
Isa. 55:1

41

*To soar like
an eagle, you
must head into
the wind.*

slowly and blend well. Pour in chicken stock and heat and stir the mixture until it reaches the boiling point. Remove the soup from the heat and rub it through a fine sieve. Add salt and white pepper to taste and set the soup aside to cool. Add the heavy cream and blend well. Chill. Garnish soup-filled bowl with asparagus tips or green pepper rings and sprinkle with paprika. If desired, soup bowl can be set in a partially ice-filled bowl for serving.

HOLIDAY FRUIT SOUP

1 cup dried apples
1 cup raisins
Cinnamon-sugar to taste
5 cups water
1 can (1 lb.) jellied cran-
    berry sauce, about 2 cups

1 can (12 oz.) apricot nec-
    tar
1 bottle (1 pt.) cranberry
    juice cocktail
Love
Patience

Place dried apples, raisins, and 2 or 3 generous dashes of cinnamon-sugar in a saucepan with 5 cups of water. Cook over medium heat for 25–30 minutes. While dried fruits are cooking, place cranberry sauce into a kettle and mash with a fork until sauce is smooth. Put over low heat and add apricot nectar. Continue to heat and stir. When apples and raisins are tender, mix them with the cranberry mixture and cook about 15–20 minutes. Remove from heat and allow to stand for about 15 minutes so that the flavor may be evenly distributed. Pour soup sauce through a colander into serving bowl. Mash pulp to remove all the natural juices. Soup may be served hot or cold. Just before serving, stir in cranberry juice cocktail and mix well. Serves 4–6.

COCONUT SOUP POLYNESIAN

1 cup milk
2 fresh coconuts, grated
  (or 2 cups frozen moist-
  type shredded coconut)
Love

3 cups clear chicken
  bouillon
2 egg yolks, well beaten
Parsley for garnish
Patience

Scald milk in a double boiler and stir in grated coconut meat. When mixture is cool, strain it through a napkin; then wring the napkin hard to force through all of the liquid. Discard the pulp. To the coconut milk, add the chicken bouillon and egg yolks and mix thoroughly. Heat the soup, but do not allow to boil. Adjust the seasoning. Serve garnished with parsley.

QUICK AND SAVORY
TOMATO SOUP

2 cans (10¾ oz. each) condensed tomato soup
¼ teaspoon sweet basil
¼ teaspoon rubbed savory
2 soup cans of water
Love

1 tablespoon minced pars-
  ley, and sprigs for garnish
Croutons
Patience

In a large saucepan mix soup, sweet basil, and savory. Then blend in the water and simmer for 15 minutes. Add minced parsley (save a few sprigs for garnish) and simmer a few minutes more. Serve hot with croutons. 4–6 servings.

43

SPICY TOMATO-CUCUMBER SOUP

5 cups tomato juice
½ cup chopped celery
4 small green onions, minced
1 tablespoon soy sauce
2 teaspoons Worcestershire powder

2 or 3 drops of Tabasco
Dash of pepper
Salt to taste
1 large cucumber, thinly sliced
Love
Patience

Combine tomato juice with celery, onions, and seasonings. Cook over medium heat for 20 minutes or until celery is tender. Remove from heat. Strain. Return smooth, clear tomato soup liquid to heat. Simmer. Add sliced cucumbers (cucumbers should never be boiled) and simmer for a few minutes. Serve hot with cucumber slices floating atop each serving. (If desired, this soup may be served cold as well as hot.) Serves 5.

And Gideon went in, and made ready a kid, and unleavened cakes of an ephah of flour: the flesh he put in a basket, and he put the broth in a pot, and brought it out unto him under the oak, and presented it. Judg. 6:19

CHICKEN AND WATERCRESS SOUP

1 cup diced cooked chicken breast
2 cups water
2 cups chicken broth
1 teaspoon salt
Love

1 teaspoon M.S.G. powder
1 tablespoon chopped onion
¼ cup diced celery
1 cup watercress, tightly packed
Patience

44

Place diced chicken in a covered saucepan. Add the 2 cups water and the chicken broth. Let simmer for 10 minutes. Add salt, M.S.G. powder, onion, and celery. Simmer until vegetables are tender. Add watercress, and bring to a boil. Serve immediately.

Salads

Is faith a rock?	*Partly*
Is faith experience?	*Partly*
Is faith blind following?	*Partly*
Is faith knowing?	*Partly*
Is faith love?	*Partly*
Is faith believing?	*Partly*
Is faith prayer?	*Partly*
Is faith worship?	*Partly*
Is faith something you can count on?	*Partly*
Is faith needed?	*Partly*
Is faith confidence?	*Partly*

What is faith?
The greatest faith is life forever in Christ.

FIESTA MELON SALAD

Cored-out melon pieces
1 fresh pineapple, cut into small chunks
1 pint of fresh strawberries, capped
Love

1 bunch of romaine lettuce, cut into small pieces
3 oranges, peeled and sectioned
1 cup mayonnaise
1 cup honey
Patience

Divide one large crenshaw melon in half (a honeydew or other melon may be used). Scoop out the centers and fill the cavities of the melons with the salad mixture tossed together.

And they gave him a piece of a cake of figs, and two clusters of raisins: and when he had eaten, his spirit came again to him: for he had eaten no bread, nor drunk any water, three days and three nights.
1 Sam. 30:12

EMERALD MOUND SALAD

2 packages (3 oz. each) lime gelatin
2 cups hot water
Dash salt
3 cans (8¼ oz. each) pineapple slices
3 tablespoons lemon juice
Cold water
1½ cups green seedless grapes
Love

Several lettuce leaves, or endive
1 cup cottage cheese, partially drained
1½ cups mayonnaise
Peach halves or pear halves, garnish
Maraschino cherries
1 cup moist coconut
Patience

Dissolve gelatin in hot water. Add salt. Drain pineapple and save syrup. Add lemon juice to pineapple syrup; add enough cold water to make 2 cups. Add syrup mix to gelatin and chill until almost set. Using a bowl-type gelatin mold, stack pineapple slices in the middle atop each other. Place grapes around outer edges of pineapple

47

rings. Pour lime gelatin over grapes and pineapple. Refrigerate, chilling until firm.

When ready to unmold dip in warm water; loosen mold and place gelatin on a platter covered with lettuce leaves or endive. In the top center, place partially drained cottage cheese. Spread on mayonnaise allowing it to roll down sides of gelatin mound almost covering it. Garnish with peach halves or pear halves, maraschino cherries, and coconut. Serves 6–8.

MIAMI FRUIT SALAD PLATTER
WITH CITRUS DRESSING

6 peach halves
1 can prunes
1 can Kadoka figs
3 bananas, thickly sliced
Love

1 package (10 oz.) frozen
  whole strawberries
½ cup pecan pieces
Mayonnaise (optional)
Patience

Arrange fruits on an attractive serving platter. Sprinkle over the fruits the pecan pieces and dot with teaspoons of mayonnaise. May be served with or without the Citrus Dressing. (If served with the dressing mayonnaise is compatible, but may be omitted if desired.)

CITRUS DRESSING:

1 cup sugar
3 tablespoons cornstarch
1 cup unsweetened pine-
  apple juice
¼ cup lemon juice

¼ cup frozen orange juice
  concentrate
Grated rind of 1 lemon
Grated rind of 1 orange

48

Combine sugar and cornstarch in a saucepan. When blended well, add unsweetened pineapple juice. Cook until mixture begins to thicken and comes to a boil. Use medium heat and keep stirring. Let the pineapple mixture boil for one minute. Remove from heat and add lemon juice, orange juice concentrate, and lemon and orange rind. Chill. Makes over 2 cups.

ARCTIC FRUIT SALAD

2 packages cream cheese
(3 oz. each)
1 cup mayonnaise
3½ cups fruit cocktail, drained
1 tablespoon honey
½ cup pecans, finely chopped
Love

½ cup maraschino cherries, chopped
2½ cups marshmallows, cut into pieces
1 cup heavy cream, whipped
2 tablespoons powdered sugar
Patience

Let cream cheese stand at room temperature to soften and then blend with mayonnaise. Mix fruit cocktail, honey, pecans, cherries, and marshmallows. Place into the refrigerator to chill and allow flavors to blend. Prepare freezer container. (Ice-cube tray, metal bowl, or cans may be used. In our menu we used cans to get round slices.)

Whip the cream, adding powdered sugar as you whip it. Combine cream cheese-mayonnaise mixture with whipped cream, then add the fruit-marshmallow-pecan mixture. Toss together and pour into containers. (A little red food coloring may be used if a pink color is desired.) Freeze until very firm—about 8 hours.

Serve in slices on lettuce leaves. (Arctic Fruit Salad

makes a beautiful dish served in an iced container.) Garnish with cheese-spread-filled celery, fresh mint, and cooked fresh asparagus spears.

COTTAGE CHEESE-CRANBERRY SALAD

Lettuce leaves
Cottage cheese
Canned cranberry sauce, sliced and chilled

Canned pear halves
Love
Patience

Place lettuce leaves on serving platter and fill the center with cottage cheese. Around the cottage cheese center, make a circle of cranberry sauce slices. Then surround that with pear halves filled with cottage cheese. Dice some cranberry sauce and sprinkle on top of the cottage cheese center.

RASPBERRY-CHEESE BOUQUET

2 packages (8 oz. each) cream cheese
¼ cup milk
1 cup red raspberry jelly
1 can (29 oz.) pear halves
Love

1 can (20 oz.) pineapple slices (optional)
Lettuce
¼ cup mayonnaise
Patience

In top of double boiler over boiling water, blend cream cheese, milk, and red raspberry jelly. When blended remove from heat and chill thoroughly. To serve, spoon over pear halves and pineapple rings (optional) in lettuce leaves and top each piece of fruit with a teaspoon of mayonnaise.

50

WALDORF SALAD GOURMET

2 cups diced celery
3 cups peeled, cored, tart apples, cut into chunky pieces
1 cup walnuts, broken pieces
Love
¼ cup raisins
2 teaspoons lemon juice
1 cup mayonnaise
1 cup commercial sour cream
2 tablespoons honey
Patience

Combine celery, apples, walnuts, and raisins. Sprinkle with lemon juice. Combine mayonnaise, sour cream, and honey. Blend together well. Mix the dressing with the prepared salad ingredients. Chill. Serves 6.

A wise old man once asked a ten-year-old girl if she could tell him where God was. Her reply was, "Can you tell me where He is not?"

GUACAMOLE SALAD

2 medium-sized, ripe avocados
2 small tomatoes, peeled and diced
1 bunch green onions, finely chopped
Love
2 tablespoons mayonnaise
¼ teaspoon garlic salt
Salt to taste
Pepper to taste
Lettuce
Patience

Peel and mash the avocados, leaving a few chunky pieces. Add all of the remaining ingredients except lettuce; mix together well. This should not be prepared too far in advance of serving, and should be covered tightly to prevent avocados turning dark. Serve on a bed of lettuce. Serves 4–6.

SALAD TRAY WITH AVOCADO DIP

2 heads lettuce	Corn chips
3 large tomatoes	Mayonnaise, or French
Avocado dip	dressing (on the side)

Quarter lettuce and place quarters at the edge of salad tray. Slice tomatoes and arrange inside the lettuce quarters. In the center place Avocado Dip. Fill in the center with corn chips. Dressing to be applied later, if desired.

AVOCADO DIP:

3 ripe avocados	Dash garlic salt
1 ripe tomato	½ teaspoon Worcester-
¼ cup mayonnaise	shire powder
2 tablespoons minced	Dash pepper
green onion	Salt to taste
1 teaspoon lemon juice	Patience
Love	

Peel and mash avocados. Peel and mash tomato removing any excess juice. Mix tomato and avocados. Add mayonnaise, onion, lemon juice, garlic salt, Worcestershire powder, pepper, and salt. Blend and mash together until mixture is of a smooth consistency. Serve promptly. Place in appropriate dip dish and place on salad tray. Surround avocado dip with corn chips.

Neither yield ye your members as instruments of unrighteousness unto sin: but yield yourselves unto God, as those that are alive from the dead, and your members as instruments of righteousness unto God.
Rom. 6:13

The sensual pleasures of this world last but for a season. Spiritual pleasures last forever.

52

ASPARAGUS SPEARS
WITH TOMATO SLICES

2 cans (15 oz. each) fancy,
   extra long, green asparagus spears
2 medium-sized tomatoes
Love

Salt
Pepper to taste
Lettuce leaves
Lemon slices, garnish
Patience

Arrange asparagus (be sure you open the cans from the bottom and lift the spears out carefully) on a tray over lettuce leaves. Slice tomatoes and arrange them on the tray. Add salt and pepper to taste. Garnish with lemon slices and serve with The New French Dressing.

Next to prayer, cooking is the greatest therapy in the world . . . while negotiating a great recipe, it is impossible to think of anything negative.

THE NEW FRENCH DRESSING

⅓ cup salad oil
2 tablespoons vinegar
2 tablespoons catsup
2 teaspoons grated onion
1 teaspoon prepared mus-
   tard
Few drops Tabasco

1 teaspoon salt
¾ teaspoon chili powder
¼ teaspoon sugar
⅛ teaspoon dry mustard
Dash pepper
Dash paprika

Combine all ingredients. Shake well in a capped jar. Recipe makes ⅔ cup.

53

CUCUMBER-TOMATO SLAW
WITH VINEGAR DRESSING

2 medium-to-large cu-
  cumbers
2 medium-to-large toma-
  toes
1 small head cabbage,
  shredded

2 radishes, shredded
2 green onions, finely
  diced
Love
Patience

Slice cleaned, but unpeeled, cucumbers. Slice tomatoes. Shred cabbage and radishes together and mix with diced onions. Arrange cucumbers and tomatoes alternately on salad plates. Finish filling the salad plates with cabbage, radish, and onion slaw. Serve with Vinegar Dressing.

VINEGAR DRESSING:

½ cup apple cider vinegar
¼ cup water
1 clove garlic, sliced
½ teaspoon salt

½ teaspoon liquid sugar
  substitute
1 teaspoon chopped chives

Combine all ingredients in a jar or bottle. Shake well. Chill. Strain out all solid pieces, for a clear vinegar dressing. Shake again before serving. Makes ⅔ cup. (This also makes an excellent diet dressing. However, the sharpness of the vinegar and extra-sweetness of the artificial sweetener makes a good combination for salad dressing anytime.)

54

SPICY RED AND WHITE SLAW

1 very large head red cabbage
1 small head red cabbage,
  shredded
1 small head white cab-
  bage, shredded
Love

1 small onion, minced
¾ cup bottled Italian-style
  salad dressing
2 tablespoons mayonnaise
Paprika
Patience

Remove core from center of large head of red cabbage
and pull back outside leaves to look like petals of a
flower. Mix shredded red cabbage, shredded white cabbage, and minced onion. Pour Italian-style salad dressing
over the cabbage mixture as you toss it together. Scoop
into the center of the cored-out cabbage. Garnish with
mayonnaise and a dash or two of paprika. (Excess salad
may be reserved in a dish and replaced as servings are
taken from the cabbage.)

*According to
my earnest
expectation
and my hope,
that in nothing
I shall be
ashamed, but
that with all
boldness, as
always, so now
also Christ shall
be magnified
in my body,
whether it be
by life, or by
death.
Phil. 1:20*

CARROT SALAD HAWAIIAN

2 cups shredded carrots
⅔ cup seedless raisins
3 tablespoons apricot nectar or frozen orange
  juice concentrate
Love

¼ cup fresh pineapple
  chunks
3 tablespoons sugar
½ cup mayonnaise
Patience

*Expectation is
one of the
greatest vibra-
tions of life. It
can fulfill or
disappoint but
without it we
live in limbo.*

Wash carrots and shred them. Add raisins which have
been plumped by soaking them in apricot nectar or
frozen orange juice concentrate. Cut up pineapple sections into chunks. Sprinkle pineapple with sugar. Toss
together with shredded carrots and raisins. Mix in
mayonnaise, and use more fruit juice for additional
moistening if wanted.

CAULIFLOWER SALAD
WITH LISBON DRESSING

1 medium-sized fresh cauliflower, or 2 packages
frozen cauliflower
flowerets
1 teaspoon salt
1 clove garlic, cut in half
1 teaspoon mixed pickling
spice

1 tablespoon lemon juice
½ cup boiling water
½ cup French dressing
Endive
1 whole fresh tomato
Love
Patience

Cook cauliflower in regular manner until crisp-tender.
Combine salt, garlic, pickling spice, lemon juice, boiling
water, and French dressing for Lisbon dressing. Arrange
cooked cauliflower on a bed of endive, centered with
whole tomato, and pour on Lisbon dressing. Serve hot
or chilled.

CORN RELISH SALAD

1 can (1 lb.) whole kernel
corn, drained
⅓ cup minced celery
¼ cup chopped green pep-
per
3 tablespoons chopped
pimiento
2 tablespoons minced
onion
Love

½ teaspoon salt
2 tablespoons salad oil
3 tablespoons vinegar
¼ cup chopped dill
pickles
½ teaspoon salad mustard
Dash of garlic salt
Dash of black pepper
Patience

56

Prepare all ingredients and thoroughly combine. Refrigerate overnight or chill thoroughly before serving.

LOTUS SALAD

2 cucumbers, peeled and
   sliced lengthwise into
   wedges
6 small stalks celery
Love

2 green peppers, seeded,
   and cut lengthwise into
   wedges
Ice
Patience

Prepare cucumbers, celery, and peppers as indicated above and chill until ice cold. Arrange on a platter on a bed of ice by alternating a cucumber wedge, a stalk of celery, and a green pepper wedge. Serve with Eastern Yogurt Dip.

We remember the fish, which we did eat in Egypt freely; the cucumbers, and the melons, and the leeks, and the onions, and the garlick. Num. 11:5

EASTERN YOGURT DIP

1 large cucumber, peeled
   and grated
1½ pints yogurt
½ medium-sized onion,
   finely chopped

1 teaspoon salt
¼ teaspoon M.S.G.
   powder
1 teaspoon cumin seed
Paprika

Grate the cucumber into yogurt. Add onion, salt, and M.S.G. powder. In a heavy, small skillet heat the cumin seeds (without oil of any kind). When seeds begin to pop up and down they are toasted properly for the recipe. Crush the seeds to a powdery consistency and mix into dip. Serve in a bowl with Lotus Salad or as a side dish for fresh raw vegetables. Sprinkle dip with paprika.

57

GOURMET SALAD

½ head romaine lettuce, cut in 1-inch pieces
½ head lettuce, pulled apart into medium pieces
½ bunch of watercress or endive, pulled apart into medium pieces
Love
2 tomatoes, quartered
12 cheese croutons (optional)
1 tablespoon garlic juice
½ cup French dressing, or more if desired
Patience

Toss all of the leafy vegetables together and arrange in a salad bowl. Mix in the quartered tomatoes and the croutons, if desired. Pour garlic juice and French Dressing over the salad and serve. Serves 4–6.

FRENCH DRESSING

1 cup water (optional)
1 cup red wine vinegar
1 teaspoon sugar
Juice of ½ lemon
2½ teaspoons salt
1 tablespoon ground black pepper
1 tablespoon Worcestershire powder
1 teaspoon English dry mustard
1 cup olive oil
3 cups salad oil

Mix all ingredients together until thoroughly blended. Chill before serving.

Let the words of our mouths and the meditations of our hearts be acceptable in thy sight, O Lord, our strength and our redeemer.

If our Lord were to return today, be sure that He would not find you in a place where you would be embarrassed or with people of whom you would be ashamed, and doing those things that would separate you from Him.

58

ITALIAN GREEN SALAD AND DRESSING

1 large head of lettuce, pulled apart into chunky sections
2 or 3 tomatoes, quartered, or tiny cherry tomatoes
Love
4–5 stalks of celery, sliced
Few tender celery leaves
½ green pepper, cut into small strips
12 ripe olives
Patience

Toss ingredients together and serve with dressing.

DRESSING:

⅔ cup salad oil
½ cup olive oil
½ cup wine vinegar
½ teaspoon salt
Dash of pepper
¼ teaspoon garlic salt
1 teaspoon oregano

Mix ingredients together and blend thoroughly. Chill before using. Makes 1⅔ cups.

LAYERED SALAD IN GLASS

¼ head red cabbage, sliced widthwise, ¼ inch thick
¼ head lettuce, sliced widthwise, ¼ inch thick
Love
2 medium-sized tomatoes, sliced
½ head romaine lettuce, whole leaves
2 hard-boiled eggs, sliced
¼ cup croutons
Patience

59

Choose a large glass container. Fill container with ingredients in order listed. Serve with Bleu Cheese Dressing. (See recipe on following page.)

BLEU CHEESE DRESSING

2 tablespoons chopped
  green onions
1 cup mayonnaise
½ cup thick sour cream
¼ cup (2 oz.) crumbled
  bleu cheese
1 garlic clove, crushed

¼ cup chopped parsley
1 tablespoon anchovy
  paste
1 tablespoon lemon juice
¼ cup vinegar
Salt
Pepper

Combine all the ingredients and season with salt and pepper to taste. Chill. Serve with Layered Salad in Glass. Recipe makes 2½ cups.

It is good for a man that he bear the yoke in his youth.
Lam. 3:27

Cakes are like children—beat them properly and they grow straight and tall.

ICED CHERRY-TOMATO GELATIN SALAD

Egg and Endive Garnish-Mayonnaise

1 package (3 oz.) cherry
  gelatin
1 cup boiling water
1 (8 oz.) can tomato
  sauce
1 cup sliced celery
¼ teaspoon salt
Dash of pepper
Dash of garlic salt
1 beef bouillon cube

⅔ cup boiling water
½ teaspoon Worcester-
  shire powder
Endive
Crushed or cracked ice
4 hard-boiled eggs
1 cup mayonnaise
Love
Patience

60

Place cherry gelatin in a mixing bowl. Pour in one cup boiling water. Stir and blend well. Add tomato sauce, celery, salt, pepper, garlic salt and mix well. Set aside while you place a bouillon cube in a cup and mix with ⅔ cup boiling water. Dissolve cube; add to cherry-tomato mixture. Add Worcestershire powder. Stir well and refrigerate.

Prepare a bed of endive on each serving dish. Scatter cracked, or crushed, ice over endive leaves. On each plate, place one-fourth of cherry-tomato gelatin, one hard-boiled egg, and top with ¼ cup of mayonnaise. Serve at once. 4 servings.

And having food and raiment let us be therewith content.
1 Tim. 6:8

RANCH BEAN SALAD

½ head lettuce, shredded
2 cans (1 lb. each) Ranch Style Beans, drained
½ cup celery, sliced
3 tablespoons chopped onions
3 tablespoons chopped green pepper
2 tablespoons chili sauce
Love

¼ teaspoon garlic salt
¼ teaspoon cracked black pepper
1 tablespoon cooking oil
1 tablespoon apple cider vinegar
Peppers, for garnish
Green pepper ring, for garnish
Patience

Arrange shredded lettuce in a salad bowl, making a bed for bean mixture. Combine all of the other ingredients except garnishes, gently tossing together. Place bean mixture onto lettuce. Garnish top with peppers and green pepper ring.

61

FESTIVE MACARONI SALAD

Our lives are like a rainbow, filled with rain and with sunshine.

4 cups cooked elbow macaroni
1½ cups sliced celery
½ cup cut-up small green onions
½ cup sliced radishes
2 tablespoons snipped parsley
1 cup mayonnaise
Love

2 tablespoons vinegar
2 teaspoons prepared mustard
½ teaspoon celery seed
1½ teaspoons salt
⅛ teaspoon pepper
Radishes, olives, or quartered tomatoes for garnish (optional)
Patience

Combine all ingredients at least two hours ahead of mealtime. Refrigerate. Garnish with radishes, olives, or quartered tomatoes. Serves 6.

HOT POTATO SALAD

2 lbs. (6 average-sized) potatoes
¼ cup bacon fat
1½ tablespoons flour
1 cup water
⅓ cup apple cider vinegar
1¾ teaspoons salt
⅛ teaspoon pepper
1 tablespoon sugar
1 teaspoon prepared mustard
Love

2 celery stalks, sliced
1 cucumber, thinly sliced
2 small onions, sliced
½ green pepper, diced
12 pimiento-stuffed green olives, sliced
Green pepper rings for garnish
Green olives for garnish
Paprika
Patience

62

Boil potatoes until barely tender. In cold 10-inch skillet over low heat, pour in bacon fat (or fry about 6 slices of bacon and remove bacon from skillet). Stir in flour, then water. Blend until smooth; add vinegar, salt, pepper, sugar, and mustard. Cook over low heat. Stir until thickened and remove from heat. When potatoes have cooked, drain, peel, and slice or dice them. Return skillet to low heat, add a layer of potatoes, then a layer of celery, then cucumber and onions, green pepper and olives, repeating till all ingredients are used. Mix together and heat through. To serve, garnish with green pepper rings, olives, and paprika. Serves 6.

CHICKEN SALAD

4 cups cooked chicken or turkey, large chunks
1 cup celery, cut on angle, small pieces
1 medium green pepper, diced, or 1 medium cucumber, diced
3 hard-cooked eggs, chopped
⅔ cup mayonnaise
¼ cup light cream
2 teaspoons grated onion
Love

1 teaspoon salt
⅛ teaspoon pepper
¼ teaspoon celery salt
½ teaspoon Worcestershire powder
3 tablespoons large pieces of green olives
¼ cup pecan pieces
Paprika
Pimiento for garnish
Green olives for garnish
Cucumber slices
Patience

Combine chicken, celery, and green pepper. Add chopped eggs. Mix together: mayonnaise, cream, onion, salt, pepper, celery salt, and Worcestershire powder. Toss dressing mixture and chicken mixture together. Add olives and pecans. Toss lightly together once more. Sprinkle paprika over top and garnish with pimiento and olives. Surround the Chicken Salad with cucumber slices. Serve with soda crackers. Serves 6–8.

SALMON SALAD

1 can (1 lb.) salmon
½ cup instant mashed po-
  tatoes, cooked
2 hard-boiled eggs, coarsely
  chopped
1 cup diced celery
½ cup mayonnaise
Love

2 tablespoons French
  dressing
1 tablespoon prepared
  mustard
Salt
Pepper
Paprika
Patience

Drain salmon and remove bones and skin. Mix well
with potatoes and add hard-boiled eggs. Add remaining
ingredients, seasoning with salt and pepper to taste. Mix
well. Chill and serve cold.

64

Meats

O Lord, thou hast searched me, and known me. Thou knowest my downsitting and mine uprising, thou understandest my thought afar off. Thou compassest my path and my lying down, and art acquainted with all my ways. For there is not a word in my tongue, but, lo, O Lord, thou knowest it altogether. Thou hast beset me behind and before, and laid thine hand upon me. Such knowledge is too wonderful for me; it is high, I cannot attain unto it. Whither shall I go from thy spirit? or whither shall I flee from thy presence? If I ascend up into heaven, thou art there: if I make my bed in hell, behold, thou art there. If I take the wings of the morning and dwell in the uttermost parts of the sea; Even there shall thy hand lead me, and thy right hand shall hold me. If I say, Surely the darkness shall cover me; even the night shall be light about me. Yea, the darkness hideth not from thee; but the night shineth as the day: the darkness and the light are both alike to thee.

Ps. 139:1–12

"Praise God from whom all blessings flow." Each day we should isolate a few moments from our demanding schedule to thank our heavenly Father for the abundant blessings that he has given us. There is not one who cannot count some treasures of the spirit or secular that are blessings today.

STEAK DURANGO

And bring hither the fatted calf, and kill it; and let us eat, and be merry.
Luke 15:23

Large sirloin steak, or other beef steak cuts
½ cup (1 stick) margarine
½ cup red wine
Juice of 1 lemon
1 tablespoon garlic salt
Love

1 teaspoon M.S.G. powder
2 tablespoons Worcestershire powder
½ teaspoon salt
¼ teaspoon pepper
Paprika
Patience

Melt margarine and mix in all other listed marinade ingredients. Place steak in a shallow pan and coat on both sides with sauce. Allow to marinate for 1 hour. Remove steak from marinade and broil to taste. During broiling process, baste with marinade. This recipe is most compatible with charcoal broiling.

STEAK BORDELAISE

These wait all upon thee; that thou mayest give them their meat in due season.
Ps. 104:27

4 slices of round steak, ¼ inch thick
Flour
1 cup (2 sticks) butter
1 onion, diced
1 green pepper, diced
1 small can mushrooms, drained
Few drops of soy sauce
Love

Few drops of Tabasco
1 teaspoon Worcestershire powder
⅓ cup of tomato sauce
3 teaspoons garlic salt
Pepper to taste
1 large can (1 lb.) English peas with liquid
Patience

Remove bones from round steaks, score around edges, and dredge in flour. Heat ½ lb. of butter in a skillet and then brown steak slightly on both sides in melted butter. Remove steak.

Using butter remaining in the skillet, sauté onions, green pepper, and mushrooms until soft. Add soy sauce,

67

Tabasco, Worcestershire powder, tomato sauce, garlic salt, and pepper. Then add large can of peas with liquid; cover skillet and allow recipe to simmer about 20 minutes or until peas are soft.

Roll up two large spoons of pea mixture in one browned piece of steak. Use toothpicks to secure steak rolls. Place steak rolls into buttered baking dish and pour remaining pea mixture over and around steaks. Cover dish and place into a preheated oven at 400 degrees. Cook for about 40 minutes or until steak is tender. Serves 4.

ROAST BEEF

(Round Roast)

And they shall eat the flesh in that night, roast with fire, and unleavened bread; and with bitter herbs they shall eat it.
Exod. 12:8

Round beef roast	Flour
Salt	2 tablespoons cooking oil
Pepper	Patience
Love	

Season roast with salt and pepper and dust with flour. In uncovered pan on top of stove heat cooking oil. Place the roast, fat side up, in the pan and sear. After the roast is well seared, turn it and sear the other side. Then place into a preheated oven at 450 degrees for about 15 minutes to brown; then reduce heat to 350 degrees and roast as long as desired. Garnish with Peach-Raspberry Garnish, page 69.

Rare: 20 minutes per pound
Medium: 25 minutes per pound
Well-done: 30 minutes per pound

PEACH-RASPBERRY GARNISH

6 canned peach halves

6 tablespoons red rasp-
berry preserves, or jelly

Spoon preserves into peach halves for garnish for roast.
This garnish recipe may also be served separately as an
appetizer.

POT ROAST WITH VEGETABLES

5 to 6-lb. boned rump pot
roast
⅓ cup all-purpose flour
2 tablespoons fat
1 teaspoon M.S.G. powder
2 teaspoons salt
⅛ teaspoon pepper
Pinch celery seed
1 tablespoon Worcester-
shire powder
Love

⅛ teaspoon oregano
3 tablespoons wine vinegar
1 medium-sized onion,
sliced
2 cups small whole white
onions
8 small carrots, pared
3 tablespoons flour
½ cup water
Patience

On wax paper roll beef in ⅓ cup flour to coat all sides.
In hot fat in Dutch oven over medium heat, brown beef
well on all sides, turning it as it browns and sprinkling
well with M.S.G. powder, salt, and pepper. This may
take 15 to 20 minutes. Add celery seed, oregano, vinegar, and 1 sliced onion. Cover tightly; simmer over low
heat, turning occasionally, about 3½ hours.

Now add the small onions and the carrots, tucking
them into gravy around beef. Cover; simmer 1 hour,
or until beef is fork-tender and vegetables are done. Remove beef and vegetables to heated platter; keep warm.

If desired, pass gravy made as follows: Skim fat from

69

broth in Dutch oven. To broth, add enough water to make 2½ cups liquid. In small bowl combine 3 tablespoons flour with ½ cup water; stir into broth. Cook until thickened. Season to taste with salt and pepper. Makes 8 to 10 servings.

SPORTSMEN'S STEW

3 lbs. lean top of rump or beef chuck, cut in 1½-inch cubes
4 tablespoons margarine
1 cup demi-glaze, or brown gravy
1 cup tomato sauce
1 teaspoon beef extract
Salt to taste
Pepper to taste
1 tablespoon Worcestershire powder
1 tablespoon chopped fresh parsley
Love

1 small bay leaf, crushed
¼ teaspoon thyme
½ cup chopped celery
2 cups carrots, thickly sliced
1 medium-sized onion, diced
3 medium-sized potatoes, quartered
1 small clove garlic, finely minced
1 can (16 oz.) green peas, drained
Patience

70

Salt and pepper beef cubes. In large, heavy kettle, melt margarine and brown beef cubes in it. When the meat is browned on all sides, add the demi-glaze, tomato sauce, and beef extract. Bring this sauce to a boil. Add Worcestershire powder, parsley, crushed bay leaf, thyme, and celery. Correct the seasoning with salt and pepper. Cover and simmer for 15 minutes. Then add carrots, onion, potatoes, and garlic. A little water may be added if sauce is too thick. Cover and simmer slowly for 2 hours or until meat is tender. Just before serving, remove the kettle from heat and let stand for 10 or 15 minutes. Carefully remove any fat that rises to the surface. Add the green peas to the hot recipe before serving. Recipe serves 6 generously.

CANTON SKILLET BEEF

¼ cup salad oil or fat
1 cup sliced onions
2 green peppers, cut in strips
1 lb. chuck roast, cut in 1-inch chunks
1 can (20 oz.) apple slices with ¼ cup liquid
1 cup water
Love

1 tablespoon Worcestershire powder
1 tablespoon soy sauce
1 teaspoon vinegar
1½ teaspoons salt
¼ teaspoon pepper
½ teaspoon M.S.G. powder
3 cups cooked rice
Patience

Start preparing recipe about two hours before supper. In hot oil in large skillet, sauté onions and green peppers until tender. Add chuck; cook until it loses its red color. Stir in apple slices with ¼ cup liquid from can, water, Worcestershire powder, soy sauce, vinegar, salt, pepper, and M.S.G. powder. Stirring occasionally, simmer, covered, 1½ hours or until meat is tender.

71

To serve: Arrange meat, with sauce, and rice on twin serving dishes. For supper, serve with big tossed salad and cheese biscuits. Makes 4 servings.

FILLET BURGERS, GOURMET

2 pounds ground beef
1 onion, diced
1 cup canned mushrooms, drained
6 drops Tabasco
2 tablespoons Worcestershire powder
Love

3 tablespoons garlic salt
Pinch of oregano
Salt to taste
Pepper to taste
6 strips bacon
Cooking oil
Paprika
Patience

Mix ground beef in a large bowl with onion, mushrooms, Tabasco, Worcestershire powder, garlic salt, oregano, salt, and pepper. Form into 6 large patties and surround each patty with a slice of bacon. Use toothpicks to secure bacon. Brush the two sides of each patty with cooking oil and sprinkle on a little paprika. Broil to taste.

To insure moist burgers, place a small piece of ice in the center of each patty when molding. As the meat broils the ice melts and the meat remains juicy. Serves 6.

POTATO BURGERS

½ lb. ground chuck
1 cup grated raw potatoes
2 tablespoons minced onion
⅛ teaspoon pepper
1 teaspoon salt
2 teaspoons Worcestershire powder

3 tablespoons fat or salad oil
½ teaspoon dry mustard
1 tablespoon snipped parsley
Love
Patience

Mix meat, potatoes, onion, pepper, salt, and Worcestershire powder. Shape into 8 patties. In hot fat in skillet, sauté patties until crisp and brown. Remove from skillet and keep warm. Add mustard and parsley to drippings in skillet; heat and then pour over patties. Makes 4 servings.

HAMBURGERS WITH A DEGREE

1½ lb. ground chuck
1 egg
2 teaspoons prepared mustard
1½ teaspoons salt
3 tablespoons butter or margarine
Dash of pepper
3 tablespoons Worcestershire powder

2¼ cups chicken broth
2 tablespoons flour
2 tablespoons bottled meat sauce
½ cup catsup
2 tablespoons snipped parsley
Love
Patience

About one hour before serving, mix thoroughly ground chuck with egg, 1 teaspoon mustard, salt, 1 tablespoon butter, pepper, 1 tablespoon Worcestershire powder, ¼ cup chicken broth. Set aside.

In a saucepan over low heat, melt 2 tablespoons butter. Stir in flour and brown. Blend in 2 cups chicken broth, 1 teaspoon mustard, 2 tablespoons Worcestershire powder, bottled meat sauce, and catsup. Simmer together, stirring until thickened.

Using a 6-ounce teacup (¾ cup) as a mold, shape meat mixture into 4 cup-shaped burgers.

Just before serving: preheat broiler 10 minutes, or as manufacturer directs. Broil burgers to medium doneness, allowing 8 minutes on rounded side, then 6 minutes on flat side. Meanwhile, reheat catsup sauce. Serve sauce in bowl garnished with snipped parsley. Makes 4 servings.

73

SUPERB SKILLET BURGER LOAF

1 egg, beaten
¾ lb. ground chuck
¾ teaspoon salt
¼ cup minced onion
Love

3 packaged process Cheddar cheese slices
¼ teaspoon pepper
Patience

About 25 minutes before supper: Mix egg, meat, salt, and onion. Grease 8-inch skillet (with metal handle); lightly pat half of meat over bottom of skillet. Arrange cheese slices on top of meat; cover with rest of meat, patting smooth. Sprinkle with pepper. Cut into 4 pie-shaped wedges. Cook on top of stove, over fairly high heat, until well-browned on bottom. Turn and brown on other side; or place the skillet under broiler until meat is nicely browned. 4 servings.

SOUTHERN BEEF LOAF

(in Potato Crust)

2 pounds ground beef
1 cup yellow corn, cooked
1 cup frozen green peas, cooked
¾ cup uncooked rolled quick oats
2 eggs
1 large onion, finely diced
1 tablespoon garlic salt
Love

2 tablespoons Worcestershire powder
Dash Tabasco
½ teaspoon oregano
1 teaspoon celery salt
Salt to taste
Pepper to taste
1 quart cooked mashed potatoes
Patience

Mix together the ground beef, corn, green peas, oats, eggs, onion, garlic salt, Worcestershire powder, Tabasco, oregano, celery salt, and salt and pepper to taste. Form this mixture into a loaf and place into a greased casserole or large baking dish. Cover dish and place into a preheated 400-degree oven and bake for 1 hour or more until the loaf is cooked through and suits your idea of well-done. Remove the loaf from the baking dish and place onto a cookie sheet that has been lightly greased. Completely coat the beef loaf with cooked mashed potatoes. Return to the oven and allow the potatoes to brown. Serve in large slices. Serves 4–6.

MEAT BALLS FINLANDIA

1 lb. ground beef	2 teaspoons catsup
¼ lb. ground veal	12 ounces grape jelly
Salt	⅛ cup water
Pepper	Parsley sprigs for garnish
1 bottle chili sauce	Patience
Love	

Combine beef and veal and roll into small meat balls. Salt and pepper lightly. In a heavy skillet combine chili sauce, catsup, grape jelly, and water. Stir together over low heat. Place meat balls into the sauce and allow to simmer until meat balls are well done and have absorbed much of the sauce (sauce will thicken). If sauce thickens too much before meat balls are done, add a little more water. Serve in a chafing dish and garnish with sprigs of parsley.

For the wages of sin is death; but the gift of God is eternal life through Jesus Christ our Lord. Rom. 6:23

None of us would think of starting an unfamiliar journey without a well-marked roadmap. Yet, some try to travel the most difficult trip, the road of life, without a guide. The Bible displays the path of comfort, courage, inspiration, strength, and sanity as we travel through our days. Then in the end, a victory . . . a direct route to eternal life.

75

MEAT-BALL STEW EN CASSEROLE

2 lb. potatoes, pared, quartered
1½ lb. small white onions
1 bunch small carrots, halved lengthwise
1 package (10 oz.) thawed frozen peas
2 lbs. ground chuck
1 egg
1 cup day-old bread crumbs
¾ teaspoon dried marjoram
2½ teaspoons salt
Love

¾ teaspoon Worcestershire powder
⅔ cup milk
⅓ cup salad oil
1½ lb. small mushrooms
1 can (10¾ oz.) condensed cream of mushroom soup
¾ teaspoon nutmeg
¾ teaspoon bottled sauce for gravy
¾ teaspoon onion salt or M.S.G. powder
Milk
Patience

In large saucepan, place vegetables in layers. In bottom of pan place potatoes, then onions, then carrots. Cook in 1-inch boiling salted water, covered, 20 minutes, or until barely tender-crisp. Top with peas; cover; turn off heat.

Meanwhile with fork, lightly mix meat with egg, crumbs, marjoram, salt, Worcestershire powder, and milk. Drop by teaspoonfuls into hot oil in skillet. Brown quickly on both sides; remove. In same skillet, sauté mushrooms until tender; remove. Then, in skillet, heat soup with nutmeg, bottled sauce for gravy, and onion salt, or M.S.G. powder.

Start heating oven to 400 degrees. Arrange drained peas, carrots, onions, mushrooms, and meat balls in a 3-quart casserole. Near edge of casserole, pour in sauce. Mash and season potatoes; arrange in mounds around edge; brush with milk. Bake uncovered 35 minutes, or until brown and bubbly. Makes 8 servings.

SWEDISH MEAT BALLS

¼ cup finely chopped
  onion
1 tablespoon margarine
½ pound ground beef
½ pound ground veal
¾ teaspoon salt
Love

Dash of white pepper
2 tablespoons flour
1 egg
¼ cup whipping cream
1 can (10½ oz.) beef con-
  sommé
Patience

Sauté onion in margarine until just tender. Combine the salt and pepper with the meats. *Beat thoroughly.* Beat in flour and egg. Beat in cream, a little at a time. Add sautéed onion. Mixture should be light and fluffy. Form into small (about 1-inch round) balls and lightly brown in additional margarine. Toss balls around by shaking skillet. Remove surplus fat and add consommé. Cook uncovered about 15 minutes. Makes about 24 meat balls.

If then God so clothe the grass, which is today in the field, and tomorrow is cast into the oven; how much more will he clothe you, O ye of little faith?
Luke 12:28

MEAT BALLS MILANO

1 lb. ground beef
1 cup fresh bread crumbs
⅓ cup Italian dressing
1 egg, beaten
Love

2 tablespoons chopped
  onion
½ teaspoon salt
Dash pepper
Salad oil
Patience

It is no disgrace to be poor. It is a disgrace to stay that way.

77

Combine all ingredients, except salad oil; mix lightly. Shape into balls; brown in oil. Cover and simmer 15 to 20 minutes. Serves 4.

ITALIAN SPAGHETTI
WITH MEAT SAUCE

2 tablespoons bacon fat
½ cup chopped onion
½ cup chopped green
  pepper
1 lb. ground chuck
1 can (6 oz.) of button
  mushrooms, with liquid
½ teaspoon garlic salt
1 large can tomatoes
  (about 3 to 3½ cups)
1 can (8 oz.) tomato
  sauce
3 tablespoons catsup
1½ teaspoons salt
⅛ teaspoon pepper
Love

1 teaspoon sugar
¼ teaspoon cinnamon
3 tablespoons dark corn
  syrup
1 teaspoon Worcestershire
  powder
Dash or two Tabasco
½ teaspoon oregano
¼ teaspoon M.S.G.
  powder
½ teaspoon paprika
1 lb. extra long spaghetti
3 tablespoons Parmesan
  cheese
½ cup Parmesan cheese
Patience

For we walk by faith, not by sight.
2 Cor. 5:7

Avoid trouble by being too busy to worry, loving too much to anger, and having too much faith for fear.

Pour bacon fat into extra large, heavy skillet. Sauté onion and green pepper in fat until tender. Add ground chuck and cook until slightly browned on all sides. Add mushrooms and mushroom liquid. Stir, and allow to simmer. Add all other ingredients except spaghetti and Parmesan cheese and continue to simmer. (If more liquid is needed you may add water or more tomato sauce.) Cook uncovered. Turn ingredients over, especially the beef, several times.

In a large kettle cook spaghetti according to directions on package. Drain and return to kettle. Pour the meat sauce over spaghetti. Add 3 tablespoons Parmesan cheese. Toss together until flavor of meat sauce is distributed throughout the spaghetti. This will require simmering for about 15 minutes. Serve topped with Parmesan cheese. Serves 6–8.

78

SPAGHETTI WITH SAUCE ITALIA

SPAGHETTI:

4 quarts boiling water
2 tablespoons salt

1 package (1 lb.) long
spaghetti

SAUCE ITALIA:

1 onion, chopped
1 garlic clove, minced
1 tablespoon olive oil
1 cup tomato juice
1 cup meat broth
½ teaspoon minced
parsley
½ teaspoon M.S.G.
powder

Salt
Pepper
2 tablespoons grated Parmesan cheese
Pimiento, for garnish
Tiny cocktail onions, for
garnish
Love
Patience

Without self-discipline we are as unstable as a bowl of jello.

Bring the 4 quarts of water with 2 tablespoons salt to a boil and place the spaghetti in the water. Let it continue boiling for about 15 minutes, until soft. Drain in a colander and let cool water run through spaghetti for a few seconds.

Sauté the onion and garlic in the olive oil. When the onion turns a golden color add tomato juice, meat broth, and parsley. Season with M.S.G. powder, salt, and pepper to taste. Simmer. Mix in grated Parmesan cheese. Blend well. Pour one-half of the sauce onto spaghetti and toss together well. Place spaghetti into serving bowl and pour the rest of the Sauce Italia over the top. Garnish with pimiento and tiny cocktail onions.

79

STUFFED CABBAGE

1 large head cabbage
1 lb. ground chuck
½ cup uncooked regular
 or processed white rice
1 small onion, grated
2 eggs
1 teaspoon salt
¼ teaspoon pepper
1 large onion, sliced
2 small cans (8 oz. each)
 tomato sauce

2 large cans (29 oz. each)
 tomatoes (7 cups)
Juice of 2 lemons
1 teaspoon salt
¼ teaspoon pepper
½ to 1 cup brown sugar,
 packed
Love
Patience

Common sense and logic are the lighthouses that warn us of danger ahead.

Remove 12 large leaves from cabbage. Trim off thick part of each leaf. Let boiling water stand on leaves a few minutes, so they become easy to roll.

Combine meat, rice, onion, eggs, 1 teaspoon salt, and ¼ teaspoon pepper. Place mound of meat mixture in cup part of each leaf. Loosely fold over sides of each leaf; roll up.

Start heating oven to 375 degrees. In bottom of Dutch oven, place a few of remaining cabbage leaves. Arrange layers of stuffed cabbage, with seam sides down, and sliced onion in Dutch oven. Pour on tomato sauce, tomatoes, and lemon juice. Add 1 teaspoon salt, ¼ teaspoon pepper. Bring to boil on top of stove. Sprinkle with sugar to taste. Bake, covered, 1 hour; uncover; bake 2 hours. Makes 8 servings.

TEXAS CHILI CON CARNE

4 tablespoons shortening
2 pounds ground round
  steak
1 pound pork, cut into
  small cubes
2 cloves garlic, finely
  chopped
1 large onion, finely diced
3 tablespoons chili powder
Love

1 tablespoon flour
1 can (1 lb.) tomatoes
2 bay leaves
1 teaspoon oregano
1 teaspoon salt
2 teaspoons cumin seed
½ teaspoon coriander
1 small block (1 oz.) bitter-
  sweet chocolate
Patience

And the house of Israel called the name thereof Manna: and it was like coriander seed, white; and the taste of it was like wafers made with honey.
Exod. 16:31

Place shortening in large skillet and over low heat brown the ground round, pork, garlic, and onions. When the meat is brown and the onions and garlic are soft, add the chili powder blended with the flour. Press the tomatoes through a fine sieve and add to the meat. Mix in bay leaves, oregano, salt, cumin seed, and coriander. Simmer slowly for 2 hours. During the simmering process, add the bitter-sweet chocolate. For thinner chili, add water or tomato juice. Serve garnished with tamales, olives, and grated cheese. Recipe makes 1 quart.

FRIJOLES

Dried Beans

This is a great combination item for Texas Chili con Carne. Frijoles, or beans, are as important to Mexican cuisine as tortillas. They are served at almost every meal, including breakfast, and they find their way into many appetizers, tacos, tostadas, and such. The Mexican way of cooking them is quite a project; after the beans are boiled tender they add them, a few at a time and along with some bean liquid, to some fat in a frying pan, mashing them until all are used.

81

VEAL PARMIGIANO

1 lb. thin veal cutlets
3 tablespoons olive or salad oil
3 cloves garlic, finely minced
1 onion, minced
2½ cups canned tomatoes
1¼ teaspoon salt
¼ teaspoon pepper
1 can (8 oz.) tomato sauce
Love

¼ teaspoon dried thyme
1 egg
¼ cup packaged dried bread crumbs
½ cup grated Parmesan cheese
3 tablespoons olive or salad oil
½ lb. mozzarella or muenster cheese
Patience

Ask meat man to cut veal into 8 pieces of about 4½ x 2-inch size. In 3 tablespoons hot olive oil in saucepan, sauté garlic and onion until golden. Add tomatoes, salt, pepper; break up tomatoes with spoon; simmer, uncovered, 10 minutes. Add tomato sauce and thyme; simmer, uncovered, 20 minutes.

Beat egg well with fork. Combine crumbs and ¼ cup Parmesan cheese. Dip each veal piece into egg, then into crumbs. Sauté 3 pieces in 1 tablespoon hot olive oil in skillet, turning once, until golden brown on both sides. Repeat until all are done. Set slices, side by side, in baking dish 12 x 8 x 2-inches.

Start heating oven to 350 degrees. Thinly slice mozzarella cheese. Pour ⅔ of tomato mixture over veal, straining it, if desired. Arrange mozzarella cheese on top; spoon on rest of tomato mixture. Sprinkle with ¼ cup Parmesan cheese. Bake, uncovered, 30 minutes. Makes 4 generous servings.

82

SWEET-AND-SOUR PORK CHOPS

4 pork chops, 1-inch thick	1 medium green pepper,
2 tablespoons flour	cut in small strips
1 teaspoon salt	1 medium onion, sliced
1 tablespoon cooking oil	2 tablespoons molasses
1 can (4 oz.) mushrooms,	2 teaspoons soy sauce
with liquid	2 tablespoons vinegar
Love	Patience

Sprinkle pork chops with flour combined with ½ teaspoon salt. Brown chops in cooking oil in a skillet. Drain mushrooms but save liquid. Measure liquid and add enough water to make 1 cup. Add liquid and mushrooms to pork chops with green pepper and onion. Sprinkle with remaining ½ teaspoon salt. Combine molasses, soy sauce, and vinegar. Add to skillet. Cover and cook over low heat 45 minutes. Recipe serves 4. (Serve surrounded by Candied Sweet Potatoes.)

Train up a child in the way he should go: and when he is old, he will not depart from it. Prov. 22:6

The greatest place to teach children love, faith, creativity, how to work, and science is in the kitchen.

CANDIED SWEET POTATOES

2 tablespoons butter	Salt to taste
1 can (16 oz.) sweet po-	½ cup brown sugar
tatoes, with liquid	

Melt butter in a skillet and add the sweet potatoes with liquid from the can. Salt. Sprinkle the brown sugar over the potatoes. Gently turn potatoes over several times until candied (about 15 minutes).

83

DELTA PORK-CHOP CASSEROLE

4 loin pork chops, ¾-inch thick
Seasoned salt
½ cup uncooked regular or processed white rice
1 can (10¾ oz.) beef gravy (1¼ cups)
Dash Tabasco
Love
¼ cup water
1 teaspoon salt
Dash pepper
4 medium-sized onions, sliced
2 large carrots, cut on angle into 1-inch slices
Patience

About 1½ hours before dinner: start heating oven to 350 degrees. Trim bit of fat from chops and heat in skillet. Rub skillet with the fat. Sprinkle chops generously with seasoned salt; then brown well on both sides in hot skillet. Remove chops to 2-quart casserole. Add rice to drippings in skillet and cook, stirring, until browned. Stir in gravy, Tabasco, water, salt, pepper. Arrange onions and carrots on top of chops; pour on gravy-rice mixture. Bake, uncovered, 1 hour, or until chops and vegetables are tender. Makes 4 servings.

SWEET-AND-SOUR SPARE RIBS

4 pounds spare ribs
Juice of 2 lemons for marinade
1 bottle (14 oz.) catsup
½ cup white syrup
⅓ cup wine vinegar
Juice of 1 lemon for sauce
Love
1 tablespoon garlic salt
Dash of Tabasco
1 teaspoon Worcestershire powder
Pineapple, for garnish (optional)
Patience

Marinate spare ribs in juice of two lemons for 30 minutes. Pour off marinade and place ribs in a greased covered oven dish. Combine remaining ingredients in a saucepan and simmer for 10 minutes, blending well. Cover the ribs with the sweet-and-sour sauce and bake, covered, at 375 degrees for 1½ hours. Check ribs from time to time and baste with sauce. Do not allow ribs to become dry. They should be moist and tender. Remove the lid for the last 10 minutes. Garnish with pineapple and serve hot.

HAM SCANDINAVIAN

14-pound ham
1 jar (1 lb.) honey
1 cup brown sugar
½ cup frozen orange juice
  concentrate
Love

Apricot halves, dried
Pineapple chunks
Blueberries
Sprigs of fresh mint
Patience

Every moving thing that liveth shall be meat for you; even as the green herb have I given you all things.
Gen. 9:3

Have market man remove skin from ham. Preheat oven 10 minutes at 325 degrees. Place covered ham into oven and roast. Time for roasting should be 25 minutes to 30 minutes per pound. Ham should always be cooked well done. Remove ham from oven and score fat with a sharp knife forming crisscross lines, which will make a pattern of diamonds.

Glaze: Mix honey, brown sugar, and orange juice concentrate and spread part of glaze over ham. With toothpicks secure apricot halves, pineapple chunks, blueberries, and sprigs of mint to surface of ham. Cover fruit and mint with glaze. Place ham back into the oven and allow to glaze for about 10 minutes.

TWO-DAY CARAMEL HAM LOAF

3 cups fine fresh bread
  crumbs
2 cups milk
2 eggs
½ teaspoon salt
¼ cup nonfat dry milk
½ teaspoon dry mustard
1½ lb. round beef, ground
Love

¾ lb. uncooked (cook-
  before-eating) ham,
  ground, or 1 can
  luncheon meat, coarsely
  grated
1 cup brown sugar, packed
2 teaspoons whole cloves
2 teaspoons Worcester-
  shire powder
Patience

Start heating oven to 350 degrees. Soak crumbs in 2 cups milk for 5 minutes. With fork, beat eggs; add salt, nonfat dry milk, mustard, and meats. Toss; then, with two-tined fork, stir in crumb mixture, tossing well. Sprinkle bottoms of two 9 x 5 x 3-inch loaf pans with ½ cup brown sugar, 1 teaspoon whole cloves, and 1 teaspoon Worcestershire powder, reserving half of these ingredients for top; then firmly pack meat into pans. (Or sprinkle bottom of shallow pan with ½ cup brown sugar, 1 teaspoon whole cloves, and 1 teaspoon Worcestershire powder; place meat on top; shape into 2 flat loaves.) Sprinkle top of loaves with remaining sugar, cloves, and Worcestershire powder. Bake 1 hour. Remove from pans. Serve one loaf hot, with drippings. Refrigerate other loaf for next day. Each loaf makes 4 servings.

One loaf style: Sprinkle bottom of greased 10 x 5 x 3-inch loaf pan with ½ cup brown sugar, packed, 1 teaspoon whole cloves, and 1 teaspoon Worcestershire powder. Firmly pack meat mixture into pan. Top with remaining sugar, cloves, and Worcestershire powder. Bake at 350 degrees for 1 hour and 15 minutes. Makes 8 servings.

BROILED HAM SLICES
WITH APPLE AND PINEAPPLE RINGS

2 ham slices, ¾ inch thick
1 large can (20 oz.) pine-
    apple slices
3 apples, peeled, cored,
    and sliced in rings

Maraschino cherries (op-
    tional)
Love
Patience

Score edges of ham slices about ¼-inch deep in several places. (This keeps ham from cupping when it is broiled.) Broil 10–12 minutes on one side. Turn and broil 10–12 minutes on the other side. Place pineapple slices and apple rings on broiler rack surrounding ham slices. If desired, add maraschino cherries. Place foods about 3 inches from heat. Broil 5 minutes. Turn ham and fruit. Baste with ham juice (or butter). Broil 5 minutes more. Serves 4.

A child of God is soon to forgive as he realizes the value of time. Forgiveness is a key to health, happiness, and the door of heaven.

ROAST LEG OF LAMB

Select leg of lamb and place fat side up in a roasting pan on rack. Do not cover. The oven should be set at 325 degrees. Roast 30 to 35 minutes per pound. If a meat thermometer is used it should register 175 degrees for medium-done and 180 degrees for well-done. If fat on the leg is very thin, place a couple of strips of bacon over the top of fat side or cut side. Serve on platter with Boiled Onions and Carrots, garnished with sprigs of mint, cherries, and crabapples, and with Gravy of Lamb. Recipes are on the following page.

87

BOILED ONIONS AND CARROTS

8 medium-sized onions
1 bunch large carrots, cut
   in thick sections
Salt
Love

Pepper
¼ teaspoon M.S.G.
   powder
Patience

Into three cups of boiling water which has been salted, place the onions and carrots. Add M.S.G. powder. Boil the vegetables until just tender—about 15 minutes. Remove from water. Place on platter with Roast Leg of Lamb. Serve with Gravy of Lamb.

Speak ye unto all the congregation of Israel, saying, In the tenth day of this month they shall take to them every man a lamb, according to the house of their fathers, a lamb for a house.
Exod. 12:3

GRAVY OF LAMB

Meat drippings
2 cups hot water
3 tablespoons onion, finely
   chopped
4 tablespoons flour

1 teaspoon gravy seasoning
   (Kitchen Bouquet)
½ teaspoon M.S.G.
   powder
Salt
Pepper

When meat is removed from the roasting pan, take 4 tablespoons of meat drippings out of pan and put into small bowl. Add hot water to drippings remaining in pan and simmer over low heat. Add onion. Pour gravy mixture into a saucepan and keep on low heat. Mix flour with drippings in bowl. When blended, combine with gravy mixture in saucepan. While stirring, bring to a boil and add gravy seasoning and M.S.G. powder. Taste and adjust seasonings by adding salt and pepper. Simmer and keep hot until ready to serve.

LAMB JERUSALEM

3 pounds lamb shoulder, cut into 2-inch cubes
¼ cup flour
2 cloves garlic, sliced
4 large onions, sliced
¾ cup margarine
4 small apples, pared, chopped
4 tablespoons curry powder
4 tablespoons brown sugar
4 tablespoons raisins
Love

4 tablespoons Worcestershire powder
2 lemons, sliced
4 tablespoons shredded coconut
¾ cup chopped walnuts
½ teaspoon lime peel
1 tablespoon salt
2 cups water
2 apples, cut into wedges, for garnish
Rice
Patience

A clove of garlic and a happy smile speak all languages.

Roll the lamb cubes in the flour. Sauté garlic and onions in margarine in a large skillet for a few minutes until lightly browned. Add lamb and sauté for 10 minutes, stirring constantly. Add apples and curry powder. Simmer for 5 minutes. Keep stirring mixture and add all of the remaining ingredients except 2 apples and rice. Add two cups of water and bring to a boil. Reduce heat, cover, and simmer for 1 hour. This recipe serves 6.

Cook a generous portion of rice and serve with Lamb Jerusalem on a large serving platter or tray surrounded by Indo-side dishes.

INDO-SIDE DISHES OF VEGETABLES AND FRUIT

89

Oranges	Watermelon	Cucumbers
Limes	Apples	Potatoes
Grapes	Bananas	Tomatoes
Lemons	Eggplant	Green peppers

BROILED-SKEWERED LAMB CUBES

Lamb shoulder or neck, 2-inch cubes	4 tablespoons Worcestershire powder
Salt	Oil
Pepper to taste	Patience
Love	

Sprinkle lamb cubes with salt and pepper, and the Worcestershire powder, and coat with oil. Broil until done to your taste. Set lamb cubes on paper towel to drain and cool slightly so that you can place on skewers. Serve with bed of wild rice.

Judah, and the land of Israel, they were thy merchants: they traded in thy market wheat of Minnith, and Pannag, and honey, and oil, and balm.
Ezek. 27:17

ITALIAN PIZZA

ITALIAN TOMATO SAUCE:

1 can (1 lb.) tomatoes	Pepper to taste
4 tablespoons olive oil	Dash of sweet basil
Salt to taste	Dash of oregano

PIZZA:

1 recipe of yeast bread dough or hot roll mix	Oregano
Mozzarella cheese	Tomatoes, peeled and thoroughly drained
Sliced mushrooms	Parmesan cheese
Canadian bacon, cooked, or Italian sausage, cooked	Love
	Patience

90

Make the Italian Tomato Sauce first. Place canned tomatoes in a saucepan; add olive oil and salt and pepper to taste. Add a dash of sweet basil and a dash of oregano. Simmer slowly until sauce thickens. Set aside.

To make the Pizza, mix one recipe of yeast bread dough (or hot roll mix may be substituted) and allow to rise for 1 hour. Roll dough out flat. Place dough on a pizza pan or cookie sheet that has been lightly greased. This dough should be from $\frac{1}{8}$ to $\frac{1}{4}$-inch thick, covering the entire pan.

Top this yeast dough with part of the following ingredients: Italian Tomato Sauce, strips of mozzarella cheese, sliced mushrooms, and pieces of cooked Canadian bacon or cooked Italian sausage. Sprinkle pizza lightly with a little oregano. Then place a few spoonfuls of Italian Tomato Sauce on the top. Now break up pieces of thoroughly drained tomatoes and arrange over the surface of the pizza. Add more Italian Tomato Sauce, mozzarella cheese, mushrooms, and Canadian bacon or sausage. Sprinkle a bit more oregano on top. Then sprinkle lightly with Parmesan cheese. Bake in a preheated 425-degree oven for 20 minutes or until crust is brown and cheese melts.

And the people went about, and gathered it, and ground it in mills, or beat it in a mortar, and baked it in pans, and made cakes of it: and the taste of it was as the taste of fresh oil.
Num. 11:8

PATIO PIZZA

3 English muffins	2 tablespoons Parmesan
1 cup Italian tomato sauce	cheese
6 slices mozzarella cheese	Dash oregano
6 slices Canadian bacon	Love
1 small can sliced mush-	Patience
rooms	

91

Slice English muffins into halves and toast under a hot broiler. Spread muffins with Italian Tomato Sauce. Arrange on top pieces of mozzarella cheese, pieces of Canadian bacon, and slices of mushrooms. Sprinkle with Parmesan cheese. Place under a hot broiler and heat until the mixture is melted together. Finish with a dash of oregano to give the true Italian touch. Serve immediately.

ITALIAN TOMATO SAUCE:

1 large can (1 lb.) tomatoes	Dash of sweet basil
4 tablespoons olive oil	Oregano
Salt and pepper	

Place tomatoes in a saucepan, add olive oil, and salt and pepper to taste. Add a dash of sweet basil and oregano. Simmer slowly until sauce thickens.

WIENERS-TOMATOES-ONIONS
ON HIBACHI

1 package (1 lb.) wieners	Cooking oil
6 small tomatoes, skewered	Love
6 to 8 small onions, skewered	Patience

Make a hibachi out of a large clay flower pot and a clay flower pot base. Fill bottom of flower pot with sand. Place some charcoals on top of sand and a wire grill on top of the flower pot, or wire screening can be used. (Cut a square of it to fit over edges of flower pot.) Use a fire starter and let the charcoal burn a while before beginning to cook the wieners, tomatoes, and onions. Coat meat and vegetables with oil before cooking.

92

SAUSAGE CASSEROLE DE LUXE

8 pork sausage links
1 can (18 oz.) sweet po-
 tatoes, drained
3 medium apples, pared
1 tablespoon flour
Love

½ teaspoon salt
1 tablespoon brown sugar
¼ cup canned pineapple
 juice
¼ cup water
Patience

About 1 hour before serving: Start heating oven to 375 degrees. In large skillet, lightly brown sausage links. Into a 2-quart casserole slice sweet potatoes and apples. In small bowl blend flour, salt, brown sugar, pineapple juice, and water; pour over potatoes and apples; top with sausage. Bake 45 minutes or until apples are tender. Makes 4 servings.

A glimpse of heaven is a happy family at mealtime.

CORNY DOG CENTERPIECE

3 or 4 packages corny dogs
Cooking oil
2 large heads (heavy ones)
 cabbage
1 lb. bacon, for garnish
Love

Stuffed eggs (optional)
Mustard to place atop the
 corny dogs
Parsley, for garnish
Patience

Cook corny dogs according to package directions, using cooking oil. Stick cooked corny dogs into the heads of cabbage so they will stand upright and be the centerpiece of the table.

Fry the bacon and drain on paper towels. Arrange bacon slices around and in between corny dogs. If desired, stuffed eggs may be included in the center food arrangement. Garnish with mustard and parsley.

93

BEAN TACOS

BEAN FILLING:

1 can (1 lb.) pork and beans
1 medium-sized onion, grated
1 tablespoon prepared mustard
1 tablespoon paprika
1 tablespoon chili powder
Love

1 scant teaspoon salt
1 scant teaspoon garlic salt
½ teaspoon black pepper
1 teaspoon Worcestershire powder
5 or 6 drops of Tabasco
Shortening
Patience

TACOS:

1 cup shortening
1 package (12) corn tortillas

Shredded lettuce
Tomato, cut in pieces

Saying, When will the new moon be gone, that we may sell corn? and the sabbath, that we may set forth wheat, making the ephah small, and the shekel great, and falsifying the balances by deceit?
Amos 8:5

The Bean Filling may be prepared in advance. Pour pork and beans onto a plate or shallow dish so that they may be partially mashed with a fork. Add all of the other ingredients except shortening and mash together. Cover the bottom of a skillet with shortening and place the bean mixture into the skillet. Cook the Bean Filling until it begins to fry. Keep stirring until the fat is absorbed.

To prepare Tacos: Melt shortening in a skillet over a medium hot heat. Place one tortilla in skillet at a time. Heat well on one side, turn and heat the other side, folding the tortilla in the middle. Hold in this position with a spatula until fried crisp. Remove and drain. Place the next tortilla in the fat and repeat the process with each one. Fill the taco with the Bean Filling. Place on shredded lettuce and tomatoes, and sprinkle the lettuce and tomato on top of the bean tacos. They may be garnished with peppers from the relish tray. Makes 12 tacos.

94

FRICASSEE OF LIVER FRANÇOISE

1⅓ cups packaged pre-
cooked rice, or 1 cup un-
cooked regular rice
5 tablespoons butter or
margarine
1 medium onion, sliced
½ lb. calf liver, cut into
3 x ½-inch strips
1 can (10¾ oz.) condensed
cream of mushroom
soup, undiluted

3 tablespoons milk
1 can (3–4 oz.) chopped
mushrooms
Dash pepper
1 can (4 oz.) pimientos,
drained, quartered
¼ teaspoon dried thyme
Snipped parsley
Love
Patience

About 15 minutes before dinner, start cooking rice as label directs. In 3 tablespoons butter in skillet, sauté onion until almost tender. Add liver; sauté with onion about 5 minutes. Add soup, milk, 3 tablespoons liquid from mushrooms, and pepper. Heat, stirring; add pimientos. Lightly sauté drained mushrooms in 2 tablespoons butter. Toss with hot rice and thyme. Onto heated platter spoon rice forming a ring. Fill with fricassee of liver. Sprinkle all with parsley. Makes 4 servings.

And my hand hath found as a nest the riches of the people: and as one gathereth eggs that are left, have I gathered all the earth; and there was none that moved the wing, or opened the mouth, or peeped.
Isa. 10:14

DEVILED EGGS IN CREOLE SAUCE

5 or 6 hard-boiled eggs
1 tablespoon softened
margarine
2 teaspoons lemon juice
¾ teaspoon prepared mus-
tard

1 teaspoon Worcestershire
powder
½ teaspoon salt
Dash of pepper
1½ tablespoons salad
dressing

95

Prepare the Creole Sauce recipe (listed below) and pour the finished Creole Sauce into a heated serving dish. Now, shell the eggs and cut into halves, length-wise. Separate the yolks and mash them. Combine yolks with all above listed ingredients. Mash and mix until the egg stuffing has a smooth consistency. Stuff egg whites with the deviled yolks. Arrange eggs on top of the Creole Sauce; cover the pan and heat over low heat until the eggs are thoroughly hot. Recipe serves 4–6.

CREOLE SAUCE:

½ cup diced green pepper
¼ cup minced onion
3 tablespoons margarine
3 tablespoons flour
½ teaspoon Worcester-
  shire powder

Dash or two of Tabasco
  sauce
2 cans (8 oz. each) tomato
  sauce
Love
Patience

Cook green pepper and onion in margarine in a skillet. Cook until tender but not brown. Blend in flour, Worcestershire powder and Tabasco sauce. Add tomato sauce. Stir well and cook until thickened. (Creole Sauce is good for fish and meat, as well as Deviled Eggs.) Makes 2 cups.

Poultry

Have courage to be ignorant of a great many things to avoid the problem of not knowing about something.

A healthy mind restricts what it absorbs. A man might contend that he has an open mind. The most open-minded place in the world is the city garbage dump. It will accept anything!

Have only thoughts of greatness and goodness and your mind will be healthy.

CHICKEN CHASSEUR

1 (2–2½ lb.) broiler-fryer,
  cut up
Flour, seasoned with salt
  and pepper ,
¼ teaspoon dried thyme
3 tablespoons butter or
  margarine
4 scallions or small onions,
  chopped
¼ lb. mushrooms,
  chopped
Love

2 teaspoons Worcester-
  shire powder
1 teaspoon sugar
1 teaspoon salt
2 tablespoons lemon juice
⅓ cup apple juice
2 tomatoes, diced
2 tablespoons snipped
  parsley
2 tablespoons snipped
  chives
Patience

Good cooks always have friends.

Coat chicken with seasoned flour to which thyme has been added. In hot butter in large skillet, sauté chicken until golden on all sides. Add scallions, mushrooms, Worcestershire powder, sugar, salt, lemon juice, apple juice, and tomatoes. Cook slowly, covered, 30 to 40 minutes or until chicken is fork-tender. Sprinkle chicken with parsley and chives. Makes 3 or 4 servings.

CHICKEN TROPICAL

1 3-lb. broiler-fryer, cut up
Flour seasoned with salt
  and pepper
½ cup shortening
1 teaspoon salt
1 cup orange juice
2 tablespoons brown sugar
Love

2 tablespoons vinegar
1 teaspoon ground nutmeg
1 teaspoon sweet basil
12 small new potatoes
1 can (29 oz.) cling peach
  slices, drained
Parsley for garnish
Patience

99

Lightly coat chicken with seasoned flour. In hot shortening, in chicken fryer or large skillet, sauté chicken until golden on all sides. Sprinkle chicken with 1 teaspoon salt. Combine orange juice, brown sugar, vinegar, nutmeg, and sweet basil; pour over chicken. Place well-scrubbed new potatoes between and around chicken pieces. Cook, covered, over medium heat, 25 minutes or until chicken and potatoes are tender. Then add peaches; heat covered for 5 minutes. Serve at once, garnished with parsley. Makes 4–6 servings.

CHICKEN IMPERIAL

12 pieces of chicken (breasts, pulley bones, thighs)
Cooking sherry
6 cups bread crumbs
2½ cups Parmesan cheese
3 cloves garlic, crushed
⅜ teaspoon pepper
Love

6 teaspoons salt
2 teaspoons flaked parsley
1½ cups chopped blanched almonds
1½ cups (3 sticks) melted butter
Parsley for garnish
Patience

Soak chicken pieces in cooking sherry for 2 hours. Mix well the bread crumbs, cheese, garlic, pepper, salt, parsley, almonds, and 1 cup of the melted butter.

Drain chicken and dip each piece in the remaining ½ cup of melted butter, then roll chicken well in the above mixture. Place the chicken pieces in an open metal pan. Put a small amount of butter on each piece of chicken. Bake for 1½ hours in a 350-degree oven. Serve warm. Garnish with parsley.

CHICKEN KIEV

½ cup (1 stick) butter or margarine
1 clove garlic, crushed
2 teaspoons snipped chives
2 teaspoons snipped parsley
½ teaspoon salt
½ teaspoon crumbled rosemary
Love

1 teaspoon Worcestershire powder
⅛ teaspoon pepper
1 egg, slightly beaten
1 tablespoon water
4½ lb. chicken breasts, boned
Shortening or salad oil
¼ cup all-purpose flour
Patience

In small bowl, combine butter, garlic, chives, parsley, salt, rosemary, Worcestershire powder, and pepper; blend well. Spread on sheet of wax paper; fold paper over top; then pat into ¾-inch thick roll. Wrap in the wax paper; freeze or refrigerate till very hard.

In bowl, blend egg and water well. Then, with rolling pin, pound each chicken breast to ¼-inch thickness. Now cut hard roll of butter mixture into four equal pieces; lay one piece on chicken breast, and roll it up in the chicken; secure with skewer or string. Repeat.

In Dutch oven, heat 1½ inches of shortening or salad oil to 370 degrees on deep-fat-frying thermometer, or until square of day-old bread browns in 60 seconds. Meanwhile, dip chicken rolls in flour, then in egg mixture, then in flour. Now, with tongs, lower two chicken rolls into hot fat; fry about 15 minutes, turning occasionally; then drain on paper towels. Repeat. Remove skewers or string; serve hot. Makes 4 servings.

Serve on bed of fluffy wild rice.

So Naomi returned, and Ruth the Moabitess, her daughter in law, with her, which returned out of the country of Moab: and they came to Bethlehem in the beginning of barley harvest.
Ruth 1:22

101

SAUTÉED (BRAISED) CHICKEN

1 cut-up or quartered small broiler-fryer. Or chicken parts. Allow ¾ to 1 lb. per serving.
Flour
Love

3 to 4 tablespoons butter or cooking oil
½ cup liquid (water, bouillon, or tomato juice)
Patience

Dust cut-up chicken lightly with flour, if desired. In large skillet or chicken fryer, heat 3 to 4 tablespoons butter or cooking oil until bubbling. In it, brown chicken, uncovered, quickly but well on all sides, turning with tongs. (If you're cooking 2 chickens, use 2 skillets, one for meaty and one for less meaty pieces.)

When chicken is nicely browned, turn heat low. Then add ½ cup liquid and any of these seasonings:

Dried or fresh basil, thyme, or rosemary
Minced celery
Curry powder
Garlic, celery, or onion salt
Minced green pepper
M.S.G. powder
1 teaspoon Worcestershire powder

Sliced and lightly floured mushrooms
Minced onion, chives, shallots or garlic
Minced pimiento
Salt and pepper
Seasoned salt

Now cover skillet. Let chicken cook slowly, turning it occasionally to cook evenly, 25 to 30 minutes or until fork-tender. For crisp-crusted chicken, uncover last 10 minutes. Just before removing chicken to platter, sprinkle with snipped parsley and paprika. Arrange chicken on heated platter and pour pan juices over all.

102

COUNTRY CHICKEN
BAKED IN CREAM

1 frying chicken
1 teaspoon salt
½ teaspoon white pepper
½ teaspoon celery salt
Love

½ cup flour
4 tablespoons butter or
  bacon fat
1½ cups sweet cream
Patience

Cut the chicken in serving pieces. Sprinkle with salt, pepper, and celery salt. Roll in flour. Brown on both sides in butter or bacon fat. Pour cream over the chicken. Cover and put in the oven. Bake for 1 hour at 375 degrees. Serve with cream gravy.

ROAST CHICKEN

1 or 2 3-lb. ready-to-cook
  broilers
1 teaspoon salt for each
  chicken
¼ teaspoon pepper for
  each chicken

Cooking oil
¼ teaspoon paprika for
  each chicken
Love
Patience

Wash chickens inside and outside with damp cloth. Sprinkle chickens inside with salt and pepper and rub in some oil. (For a roasted chicken that looks its prettiest, skewer opening shut and lace with cord. Fold neck skin over and fasten to the back with a skewer. Tie wings across back and tie drumsticks to tail with cord.) Place chicken with breast side up on a rack and place into a shallow roasting pan. Brush with oil, sprinkle with salt, pepper, and paprika. Roast uncovered in 400-degree oven 45 minutes or until tender. Baste often with drippings.

And not only so, but we glory in tribulations also: knowing that tribulation worketh patience.
Rom. 5:3

How long it takes to learn patience . . .

During the anxious twenties, nothing will happen soon enough. The adjusting thirties is a time we spend searching. Finally, we arrive at the patient forties. By now we have learned to face and to handle trials and tribulation. The virtue we are rewarded is patience.

103

CHICKEN TETRAZZINI

1 6-lb. hen
2 teaspoons salt
½ teaspoon pepper
1 pound Italian-style thin
  spaghetti
½ cup (1 stick) butter
2 medium-sized green pep-
  pers, finely chopped
5 tablespoons flour
2 cans (10¾ oz. each) condensed cream of mush-
  room soup
2 cups milk
2 small jars pimiento
¼ teaspoon garlic salt
1 clove garlic, minced
1 tablespoon Worcester-
  shire powder

½ cup cooking sherry
2 large cans (8 oz. each)
  button mushrooms,
  drained
6 cups grated process
  American cheese
¾ cup Parmesan cheese
1 cup finely chopped al-
  monds
1 small can (2 oz.) button
  mushrooms, drained
Olives (optional)
Pimiento (optional)
Endive (optional)
Slivered almonds (op-
  tional)
Love
Patience

Cover hen with water. Add salt and pepper. Cook slowly 3 hours or until meat loosens from the bones. Save broth. Remove meat from bones and dice into small pieces. Cook spaghetti in boiling chicken broth until tender. Drain and rinse. Melt butter over low heat in large pan. Add green peppers to butter and cook until tender. Add flour, mushroom soup, milk, chopped pimiento, garlic salt, garlic clove, Worcestershire powder, cooking sherry, mushrooms, diced chicken, 4 cups of the American cheese, and Parmesan cheese.

Cook slowly for 10 minutes. Place layer of spaghetti in buttered casserole. Cover with a layer of sauce. Continue the process until the dish is nearly filled. Sprinkle chopped almonds and remainder of grated American cheese on top. Place button mushrooms on top of the cheese. Bake for 10 minutes in preheated 350-degree

104

oven. If desired, garnish with olives, pimiento, endive, and slivered almonds. Serve while hot.

HUNTER'S SAUTÉED QUAIL

6 club rolls
¾ cup butter
6 quail, split
1 teaspoon salt
Love

Freshly ground black
  pepper
Fruit Sauce
Patience

Split rolls in half and hollow out centers. Toast in a 325-degree oven until brown. Melt ¼ cup butter and brush the rolls with the butter. Sauté the quail over high heat in the remaining ½ cup of butter for 10 minutes or until golden brown. Sprinkle quail with salt and pepper. Arrange quail on rolls and serve with Fruit Sauce. Serves 6.

FRUIT SAUCE

1 cup seedless white grapes
1 cup water
4 tablespoons butter
¼ cup bottled grape juice
⅛ teaspoon ground cloves

½ teaspoon ginger
2 tablespoons finely
  chopped mushrooms
½ cup finely chopped
  hazelnuts

Bring grapes and water to a boil. Cover, reduce heat, and simmer for 5 minutes. Drain off water. Add butter, grape juice, cloves, and ginger. Cover and simmer for 5 minutes. Stir in mushrooms and simmer for 5 minutes. Add hazelnuts and serve immediately. Makes about 2½ cups.

STUFFED PHEASANT PIECES

8 pheasant pieces
Flour
Salad oil or shortening
Love

3 teaspoons cornstarch
1 tablespoon water
Patience

MARINADE:

¼ cup soy sauce
½ cup chicken broth
1 tablespoon honey

1 clove garlic, minced or
   mashed
1 teaspoon grated fresh
   ginger root

STUFFING:

1 cup chicken livers,
   cooked and mashed fine
2 tablespoons finely
   chopped dill pickles
2 tablespoons finely
   chopped green onions

2 tablespoons finely
   chopped green pepper
1 tablespoon chopped
   pimiento
⅛ teaspoon ground
   celery seed
⅛ teaspoon cayenne pep-
   per

Bone pheasant pieces; remove skin and gristle. Marinate about 30 minutes in a marinade of soy sauce, chicken broth, honey, garlic and ginger root. Meanwhile, combine all stuffing ingredients.

When pheasant pieces have marinated, drain well, reserving marinade; then roll about a tablespoon of stuffing mixture into each. Fasten with skewers or string, roll in flour, and brown in hot shortening.

When they have become nicely browned, place in 1-quart shallow casserole. Add about ⅔ cup marinade; cover and bake 25 minutes in a 375-degree oven. Mix together cornstarch and water; add remaining marinade and pour over pheasant pieces. Return pheasant pieces to oven uncovered and bake 15 minutes longer. Serve with steamed rice and a tossed green salad. Makes about 4 servings.

Seafood

If you can command ten great sauces, you are truly an outstanding cook.

If you are commanded by God's Ten Commandments, you are truly an outstanding person.

MANHATTAN CLAM CHOWDER

6 strips bacon
4 medium-sized onions, diced
4 carrots, finely diced
1 small stalk celery, finely chopped
2 tablespoons chopped fresh parsley
1 pint clams (2 10½-oz. cans may be used)
Love

1 can (14½ oz.) tomatoes
1 bay leaf
2 teaspoons thyme
1 tablespoon Worcestershire powder
Salt
Cracked black pepper to taste
3 medium-sized potatoes, finely diced
Patience

For if ye forgive men their trespasses, your heavenly Father will also forgive you: But if ye forgive not men their trespasses, neither will your Father forgive your trespasses.
Matt. 6:14–15

Cut bacon into small pieces and fry in a large kettle until brown, but not crisp. Add onions and sauté until soft. Next add carrots, celery, and parsley. Simmer slowly for about 4 minutes while stirring. Drain clams and tomatoes, placing the liquid into a measuring container. Add enough water to make about 1½ quarts of liquid. Add tomatoes and liquid to the pot and bring to a boil. Season with bay leaf, thyme, Worcestershire powder, salt and pepper. Reduce heat and simmer chowder for about 45 minutes. Add potatoes and simmer for 20 more minutes. Last, add the clams and simmer gently for 10 more minutes. Makes about 3 quarts.

MAINE BROILED LOBSTERS

2 (1-lb. size) live lobsters
Butter, melted
Salt
Pepper
Love

1 teaspoon Worcestershire powder
Paprika
Lemon wedges
Patience

109

To kill lobster: lay lobster on back shell on wooden board. To sever spinal cord, insert point of knife

And they gave
him a piece of
a broiled fish,
and of an
honeycomb.
Luke 24:42

through to back shell where body and tail of lobster come together.

With sharp knife split body of lobster down middle, cutting through thin undershell just to back shell and leaving back shell intact. Discard dark intestinal vein running down center of lobster; also discard small sac below head. Crack large claws. Lay lobsters on back shells on broiler rack; spread open. Brush with melted butter; sprinkle with salt, pepper, Worcestershire powder, and paprika.

Broil, 4 inches from heat, 12 to 15 minutes, or until lightly browned. Serve with lemon wedges and melted butter.

JAMBALAYA

½ cup diced salt pork
½ cup diced ham
½ cup chopped onion
1 clove garlic, crushed
1 tablespoon diced green pepper
2 cups (1 17 oz. can) canned tomatoes
1 red pepper pod, chopped
Love

2 tablespoons chopped parsley
½ bay leaf, crushed
1 cup uncooked rice
2 cups water
1 teaspoon salt
1 pint oysters with liquor
1 pint peeled and deveined raw shrimp
Patience

Place into skillet salt pork and ham; then fry the pork and ham slowly over low heat until crisp. Add onion, garlic, green pepper and sauté until soft. Add tomatoes, red pepper pod, parsley, and bay leaf; simmer, stirring slowly until thick. Then add rice, water, and salt. Cover skillet and simmer mixture slowly for about 10 minutes. Add oysters and shrimp. Cook slowly until rice is tender. Serves 8.

GALVESTON FRIED OYSTERS

Salad oil or shortening for
  frying
2 eggs, beaten
¼ cup liquid from oysters
Love

½ teaspoon salt
½ teaspoon pepper
3 dozen fresh oysters
Cracker crumbs
Patience

In a large, heavy skillet, heat salad oil (at least one inch deep) to 375 degrees on deep-frying thermometer. Combine eggs, liquid from oysters, salt, and pepper. Dip oysters in cracker crumbs, then in egg mixture, coating completely. Dip oysters again in cracker crumbs. Fry, a few oysters at a time, until golden on both sides— about 3 minutes in all. Drain well on paper towels. Makes 4 to 6 servings.

NEBRASKA SCALLOPED OYSTERS

¼ cup butter
¼ cup light cream
½ teaspoon salt
⅛ teaspoon pepper
½ teaspoon Worcester-
  shire powder
2 tablespoons snipped
  parsley
½ teaspoon lemon juice
Love

1¼ cups coarsely broken
  saltines
½ cup grated process
  Cheddar cheese
2 dozen shucked oysters,
  drained (1 quart)*
1 can (12 oz.) whole kernel
  corn, drained
Patience

Heat oven to 400 degrees. In small saucepan, combine butter, cream, salt, pepper, Worcestershire powder, parsley, and lemon juice. Heat just long enough to melt butter.

    Meanwhile, in greased 10 x 6 x 2-inch baking dish, arrange half of saltines. Over crackers, sprinkle cheese;

111

on top, arrange oysters and corn. Pour butter mixture over all; then sprinkle with remaining cracker crumbs. Bake 20 to 25 minutes. Serve immediately. Makes 4 to 5 servings.

* With fingers, pick over oysters to remove bits of shell.

SCALLOPS BAKED IN SHELLS

¾ cup water
½ teaspoon salt
Few grains cayenne
1 pint sea scallops
2 tablespoons butter or margarine
1 small onion, minced
2 tablespoons flour
½ clove garlic, minced
Love

1 teaspoon Worcestershire powder
1 teaspoon snipped parsley
1 egg yolk, well beaten
¾ cup buttered tiny fresh bread crumbs
2 tablespoons grated Parmesan cheese
Patience

Heat oven to 425 degrees. In skillet, combine water, salt, cayenne. Add scallops and simmer for 5 minutes. Drain, reserving liquid. Coarsely chop scallops (or try snipping them with kitchen shears).

In hot butter in same skillet, sauté onion until tender; stir in flour and mix well. Stir in reserved liquid and cook until thickened. Add garlic, Worcestershire powder, and parsley. Then, stirring constantly, cook 5 more minutes.

Gradually stir some of sauce into beaten egg yolk; then, into remaining sauce, slowly stir in egg yolk mixture. Add scallops and heat gently.

112

Into 5 buttered 6-inch pie plates or into scallop shells, spoon scallop mixture. Top with crumbs and Parmesan cheese. Bake until brown, about 5 minutes. Makes 5 servings.

SHRIMP WITH PEPPERS

6 tablespoons unsifted all-purpose flour
2 tablespoons grated Parmesan cheese
1¾ teaspoons salt
1 teaspoon Worcestershire powder
Love

1 pound raw shrimp, shelled and deveined
½ cup olive or salad oil
1 clove garlic, crushed
6 medium-sized green peppers, cut into strips
Dash pepper
Patience

Mix together flour, Parmesan cheese, 1 teaspoon salt, and Worcestershire powder. Toss shrimp in mixture, coating well. Slowly heat oil in large, heavy skillet. Add shrimp and garlic. Cook about 5 minutes, or until shrimp are golden. Remove shrimp from skillet and set aside. Add pepper strips to skillet. Cook, covered, over medium heat, 10 to 15 minutes, or until crisp-tender. Add shrimp, rest of salt, and pepper to skillet. Cook, covered, until heated through. Drain excess oil. Serve with rice if desired. Makes 4 servings.

A simple person who lives close to God sees more on his knees than a world leader sees standing on a hill.

BAR HARBOR FISH PLATTER

6 large fillets of any desired fish
Juice of 4 lemons
Tabasco
Love

2 cups mayonnaise
Paprika
6 tablespoons tartar sauce (optional)
Patience

Marinate fish for 30 minutes to 1 hour in lemon juice and a dash of Tabasco. Lightly coat fish with mayonnaise and sprinkle with paprika. Preheat broiler and broil until fish turns a golden color. Garnish with lemon slices. If desired, serve with tartar sauce.

SALMON TIMBALES

1 can (5 oz.) deveined shrimp, drained
¼ cup butter or margarine
¼ cup unsifted all-purpose flour
2 cups milk
2 cans (7¾ oz. each) salmon, drained

1 teaspoon Worcestershire powder
1 teaspoon salt
¼ teaspoon pepper
2 eggs, slightly beaten
1 tablespoon lemon juice
½ teaspoon paprika
Love
Patience

Preheat oven to 350 degrees. Lightly grease 4 6-ounce custard cups. Place 1 shrimp in center of each cup.

In medium-sized saucepan, melt 2 tablespoons butter. Remove from heat. Add 2 tablespoons flour, stirring until smooth. Gradually stir in ½ cup milk. Bring to a boil, stirring constantly. Remove from heat.

Flake salmon with fork. Add to milk mixture, with 1 teaspoon Worcestershire power, ½ teaspoon salt, the pepper, and eggs; mix well. Spoon salmon mixture in each cup over shrimp. Set cups in pan containing 1 inch hot water; bake 35 minutes.

Meanwhile, make sauce: Melt rest of butter in medium-sized saucepan. Remove from heat. Add rest of flour, stirring until smooth. Gradually stir in rest of milk; bring to a boil, stirring constantly. Reduce heat. Add lemon juice, paprika, and rest of salt. Coarsely chop remaining shrimp. Add to sauce; stir over low heat until hot.

Unmold timbales onto warm platter. Top each one with some of sauce; pass remainder of sauce.

114

RAINBOW TROUT WITH NOODLES, BUTTERED AND BREADED

3 or 4 slices bacon
3 or 4 small onions
4 or 5 small rainbow
   trout, dressed
1 bay leaf

3 teaspoons butter
1 or 2 tablespoons bread
   crumbs
Love
Patience

Place strips of bacon in the bottom of a heavy, long-handled skillet. Slice an onion and spread over bacon strips. Crumble the bay leaf and sprinkle over the onions. Place trout on this prepared cooking bed. Spread butter over trout and sprinkle with bread crumbs. Trout may be cooked over an open fire or in a 375-degree oven. Cooking time: open fire for 30 minutes; oven for 35 to 45 minutes. Turn trout over halfway through cooking time. Trout is done when it is flaky to the touch of a fork, and tender. Do not overcook as this will dry out the fish, losing much of its flavor. Serve in pan with noodles and onions for garnish.

NOODLES, BUTTERED AND BREADED:

1 package (1 lb.) noodles
Salt
½ stick butter

½ cup bread crumbs
Paprika

Cook noodles by directions on package in salted water. Drain and mix with butter. Arrange around trout and cover with bread crumbs. Sprinkle noodles, trout, and onions with paprika.

115

TROUT IN SOUR CREAM MAYONNAISE

2 large, or 4 small trout,
  boned
1 cup mayonnaise
1 cup sour cream
½ cup sugar
¼ to ½ teaspoon salt
Dash pepper
Love

Juice of ½ lemon
2 teaspoons prepared
  horseradish
⅛ teaspoon paprika
Dash garlic salt
Pinch of dill seed
Patience

Oven broil the trout until it flakes. Let cool, and then bone. Tear into medium small pieces and dip into the mayonnaise mixture. For mayonnaise mixture: Blend all other ingredients into a smooth consistency. Taste and adjust seasoning. Chill and serve cold.

TUNA AMANDINE

1 can (10½ oz.) condensed
  cream of celery soup
½ cup milk
2 tablespoons lemon juice
½ teaspoon paprika
4 drops liquid hot pepper
  seasoning
1 teaspoon Worcestershire
  powder
1 tablespoon chopped
  parsley

1 can (5 oz.) toasted slivered almonds
3 cans (7 oz. each) chunk-
  style tuna, drained
2 cups cooked sliced po-
  tatoes, drained
4 to 6 stuffed olives, sliced
2 tablespoons butter or
  margarine, melted
Love
Patience

116

Preheat oven to 350 degrees. Meanwhile, in medium saucepan, combine soup, milk, lemon juice, paprika, hot pepper seasoning, Worcestershire powder, parsley, and ¾ cup almonds. Simmer, stirring, 5 minutes.

Layer ⅔ of tuna in bottom of 2-quart casserole. Pour on ⅓ of almond sauce. Top with potatoes, then ⅓ almond sauce. Cover with remaining tuna, then remaining almond sauce.

Garnish edge of casserole with sliced olives. Fill center with rest of almonds. Pour butter over almonds; bake 30 minutes.

TUNA WITH CURRY SAUCE INTRIGUE

1 tablespoon curry powder	1 cup light cream
1 tablespoon margarine	1 cup milk
1 onion, minced	2 tablespoons cornstarch
2 stalks celery, diced	2 tablespoons cold water
½ cup sliced mushrooms	Salt to taste
1 cup diced apple	M.S.G. powder to taste
½ cup soup stock (canned chicken broth may be substituted)	2 cans flaked, white tuna
	Love
	Patience

Combine curry powder and margarine in a saucepan. Let brown. Add the onion, celery, mushrooms, and apple. Mix together well, then add soup stock. Bring mixture to a boil. Add cream and milk, and boil again. Blend together the cornstarch and cold water and add to the curry mix. Correct seasoning with salt and M.S.G. powder. Keep stirring mixture until it thickens. Makes over 3 cups.

Pour over tuna and serve hot. If desired, this sauce may be used with other fish, with rice, or chicken.

117

CODFISH CAKES

½ package (1-lb. size) salt codfish
3 medium potatoes, pared and cubed (3 cups)
⅛ teaspoon pepper
Dash ginger
1 teaspoon Worcestershire powder

1 tablespoon milk
1 egg yolk
1 small onion, grated
1 egg white
3 tablespoons butter or margarine
Love
Patience

Freshen codfish as package label directs. In large saucepan, combine codfish and potatoes with water to cover and bring to boiling. Reduce heat and simmer, covered, 30 minutes, or until potatoes are tender. Drain well.

Return codfish and potatoes to saucepan; cook, uncovered, over low heat, about 5 minutes or until mixture appears dry.

Turn codfish-potato mixture into large bowl. Add pepper, ginger, Worcestershire powder, milk, egg yolk, and onion. With wooden spoon, beat mixture vigorously about 5 minutes, or until very light and fluffy.

Beat egg white until stiff peaks form when beater is raised. Gently stir into fish-potato mixture. Shape mixture in 8 flat cakes. Sauté in hot butter, in large skillet, until golden brown on both sides. Drain well on paper towels.

Vegetables

For whom the Lord loveth he chasteneth, and scourgeth every son whom he receiveth. If ye endure chastening, God dealeth with you as with sons; for what son is he whom the father chasteneth not?

Heb. 12:6–7

I prayed for power that I might win life's game.
I was given weakness through humility so that I might learn to play . . .

I prayed for riches to fill my life with happiness.
I was given poverty to help me become wise . . .

I prayed for position to receive the praise of men.
I was given menial chores to recognize the need of God . . .

I prayed for all the best things to help enjoy life.
I was given abundant life that I would enjoy all the best things . . .

All my prayers were answered with things I had not asked . . .
Yet through God's will I am among those most richly blessed.

ASPARAGUS PARMESAN

1 bunch fresh asparagus
Salt
M.S.G. powder
Pepper
3 tablespoons butter,
  melted

4 tablespoons grated Par-
  mesan cheese
Parsley for garnish
Love
Patience

Choose young asparagus with green tips; cut off the tough ends. Cook in a small amount of salted water. Drain. Place in a shallow baking dish. Sprinkle with M.S.G. powder and pepper. Dot with butter and top with the Parmesan cheese. Brown lightly under low-heat broiler. Garnish with parsley.

Remember the sabbath day, to keep it holy. Exod. 20:8

The most popular way to observe the Sabbath is with roast, potatoes, jello, and a pro football game on TV.

ASPARAGUS ROYAL

2 packages frozen aspara-
  gus spears
½ cup (1 stick) butter
½ cup bread crumbs
¼ teaspoon M.S.G. pow-
  der
Love

1 tablespoon chopped
  parsley
Salt to taste
Pepper to taste
2 hard-boiled eggs, cut into
  halves
Patience

Cook 2 packages of frozen asparagus spears until tender. Serve covered with Royal Sauce. To prepare Royal Sauce, melt butter in a skillet and add bread crumbs. Brown the bread crumbs. Add M.S.G. powder, chopped parsley, and salt and pepper to taste. Pour Royal Sauce over the asparagus spears. Garnish with hard-boiled eggs.

121

CELERY-FRENCH GREEN BEAN MEDLEY

2 packages frozen green beans, French-cut	Dash sugar
Salt	Dash paprika
Pepper	Butter
¼ teaspoon M.S.G. powder	1 cup diced celery
	Love
	Patience

Adding salt, pepper, ¼ teaspoon M.S.G. powder, a dash of sugar, and a dash of paprika, cook green beans according to instructions on package. Dot with butter.

For preparing celery, remove the leaves and trim off all loose strings and any parts of roots. Dice. Cook celery in salted water for 15 minutes, adding pepper, a dash of M.S.G. powder, a dash of sugar, and a dash of paprika. Drain. Dot with butter. Place green beans in a serving dish and top with cooked, diced celery. If desired, add more butter.

Happy is he that hath the God of Jacob for his help, whose hope is in the Lord his God. Ps. 146:5

There is no way to obtain happiness if that is your goal. Happiness is a by-product of living a useful and honorable life.

GREEN BEANS CAROLINA

1 small can button mushrooms	4 cups (2 1-lb. cans) green beans, drained
1 can (10¾ oz.) condensed cream of mushroom soup	1 teaspoon garlic salt
¼ can (measure in soup can) milk	¼ teaspoon dill seed
	Love
	Patience

122

Blend mushrooms (retaining a few for top garnish), mushroom soup, and milk in a large saucepan. Add green beans and simmer about 10 minutes. Add garlic salt and dill seed. Mix. Continue to simmer a few more minutes. Serve hot. Makes 4 to 6 servings.

YANKEE DOODLE BEAN RING

1 can (1 lb.) Blue Lake
  green beans, whole,
  heated, drained
1 can (1 lb.) green lima
  beans, heated, drained
Green pepper strips, for
  garnish

Whole pimientos, for gar-
  nish
Salt and pepper to taste
Butter
Love
Patience

Brought beds, and basons, and earthen vessels, and wheat, and barley, and flour, and parched corn, and beans, and lentils, and parched pulse. 2 Sam. 17:28

Into a ring mold serving dish, place green beans on one side and place lima beans on the other. Where they meet, garnish with green pepper and whole pimientos. Salt and pepper to taste and place large pats of butter on beans.

GREEN BEANS AND ONIONS, TEMPURA

2 cups flour
1 egg
⅔ cup water
½ teaspoon salt
1 lb. fresh green beans,
  prepared for cooking
1 large white onion, sliced
  into rings
Love

1 bunch green onions,
  trimmed and whole
1 cup shortening or cook-
  ing oil
Soy sauce
Onion slices, paprika, and
  endive for garnish (op-
  tional)
Patience

Combine flour and egg in a mixing bowl. Blend in water and salt. Mix until batter resembles a white paste. Dip green beans and both kinds of onions into batter and fry in shortening, medium heat, until vegetables are lightly browned and crisp. Drain and serve warm with a little soy sauce. Garnish with raw onion slices, paprika, and endive.

123

SPICY GREEN BEANS

1 tablespoon chopped
  onion
2 tablespoons salad oil
½ cup chili sauce

½ teaspoon salt
1 can (1 lb.) green beans,
  drained
Love
Patience

Cook onion in salad oil until soft; add chili sauce, salt, and drained beans. Cook until thoroughly heated, stirring often.

CASHEW GREEN BEANS

2 tablespoons butter
¼ cup chopped cashew
  nuts
1 can (10¾ oz.) condensed
  cream of mushroom soup

¼ cup water
1 tablespoon minced onion
1 can (1 lb.) green beans
  (Blue Lake)
Love
Patience

Melt butter in a saucepan and lightly brown cashew nuts. Blend in cream of mushroom soup, water and minced onion. Heat slowly, but do not allow to boil. Pour over cooked green beans. Serves 4–6.

CREAMED LIMAS

2 tablespoons melted but-
  ter
½ of a large onion, finely
  diced
½ of a pimiento, finely
  diced
Love

3 cups cooked and drained
  lima beans
1 cup commercial sour
  cream
Salt to taste
Pepper to taste
Patience

124

Melt butter in skillet. Add onion and pimiento and sauté until soft. Add lima beans and allow to heat through by simmering for about 5 minutes. Mix in sour cream and add salt and pepper to taste. Recipe may be simmered for a few more minutes after the sour cream is added.

CREAM OF THE CROP BABY LIMA CASSEROLE

2 tablespoons margarine
4 medium-sized onions, sliced
1 can (6 oz.) mushrooms, drained
1 can (10¾ oz.) cream of mushroom soup
3 packages frozen baby lima beans
½ teaspoon salt
Pepper to taste

1 teaspoon dill weed
½ pt. whipping cream
1 cup grated Parmesan cheese
2 slices boiled or baked ham, slivered or diced
1 package frozen patty shells, baked
Paprika
Love
Patience

Place margarine in a skillet and melt. Sauté onions in margarine and cook until soft. Add drained mushrooms and cream of mushroom soup. In saucepan cook baby limas with amount of water called for on the package and add salt, pepper, and dill weed. Cook about 5 to 10 minutes. Drain. Place the lima beans and onion and mushroom mixture into a shallow, lightly greased baking dish, and mix together slightly.

Pour the cream over the top and sprinkle top with Parmesan cheese. Bake, uncovered, in a 300-degree oven for about 1 hour. (Don't overheat or cream may separate.) Add the ham, and serve in baked patty shells. Serve sprinkled with paprika. (Recipe may be served by spooning casserole ingredients into patty shells, if preferred.) Serves 8.

125

BEACHBOY BEANS BAKED IN TOMATOES

4 large ripe tomatoes
1 can (1 lb.) red kidney beans, drained
3 tablespoons vinegar
½ teaspoon Worcestershire powder
Dash garlic salt
Love

1 tablespoon minced onion
1 tablespoon minced parsley
3 tablespoons grated cheese
Endive, for garnish
Patience

Quarter tomatoes, but do not cut all the way through; leave bottoms slightly attached so they will open, but not fall apart. Mix all the other ingredients together. Fill the tomatoes with the bean mixture and bake in 375-degree oven for 10 to 15 minutes, until tomatoes are thoroughly heated and cheese melts into bean mixture. Garnish with endive.

RANCHERS' BEANS

1 lb. dried pinto beans
Water to cover
Salt to taste
2 tablespoons shortening

1 cup Hot Sauce
1 cup grated sharp Cheddar cheese
Love
Patience

Cook beans covered with salted water over low heat until beans are tender (4–6 hours). If necessary, add boiling water to keep beans from becoming dry. When beans are done pour off all except 1 cup water. Mash beans until smooth. Melt shortening in large skillet over low heat. Add beans and cook until slightly dry, stirring constantly. Place beans in mound on serving platter. Top with Hot Sauce and grated cheese. Makes 8 servings.

HOT SAUCE:

2 tablespoons shortening
¼ cup onion, chopped
¼ cup tomatoes, chopped
¼ cup green pepper, chopped

1 chili pepper, finely chopped
½ cup water

Melt shortening in a skillet over low heat. Add onion, tomatoes, green pepper, and chili pepper. Cook until all ingredients are soft and tender. Add ½ cup water and continue cooking for about 10 minutes. Makes about 1 cup. Serve over Ranchers' Beans.

EMPIRE STATE RED BEANS

2 cups dried red kidney beans
8 small pieces of salt pork
1 teaspoon salt
2 tablespoons butter
1 tablespoon grated onion
Love

1 tablespoon grated green pepper
2 tablespoons flour
Cracked black pepper
Dash garlic salt
Dash paprika
Patience

Cover beans with water and soak overnight. Add pork and simmer beans in soaking water for 2 hours. Drain beans; add salt and keep hot. In skillet in melted butter, sauté onion for a few seconds; add green pepper and continue to sauté for 5 to 10 minutes. Add flour, black pepper, garlic salt, and paprika and stir until well mixed. Cook until beans thicken, stirring constantly. Serves 6.

127

BAKED BEANS
IN CHAFING DISH

Prayer, like yeast, makes things happen.

4 slices bacon, each slice cut in half, making 8 pieces
2 tablespoons minced onion
2 tablespoons minced green pepper
4 cups canned pork and beans
2 teaspoons prepared mustard
2 tablespoons brown sugar
2 tablespoons dark corn syrup

1 tablespoon apple cider vinegar
3 tablespoons catsup
1 tablespoon chili sauce
Dash of garlic salt
1 teaspoon Worcestershire powder
Dash of cinnamon
Dash of allspice
Salt to taste
Pepper to taste
Paprika to taste
Love
Patience

Fry pieces of bacon until crisp. Remove from skillet and drain. Sauté the onion and green pepper in the bacon fat until tender and soft, stirring constantly. Mix onions, green pepper, and a small amount of bacon fat with pork and beans in chafing dish. Add all other ingredients, one at a time and mix. Taste. Adjust seasonings if necessary. Place chafing dish pan over hot water container and heat thoroughly. Place crisp bacon pieces on top of baked beans. Top each serving with a bacon half-slice. Serves 6–8.

PORK AND BEANS IN PEPPERS

128

6 or 8 green peppers
2 cans (1 lb. each) pork and beans
2 tablespoons catsup
Salt to taste

Pepper to taste
Paprika
2 onions, sliced, for garnish
Love
Patience

Cut the tops of the green peppers off about 1/4 inch. Core and seed them, and put into boiling water for about 5 minutes. Mix pork and beans, catsup, salt, pepper, and paprika. Remove peppers from water. Drain well.

Fill peppers with pork and bean mixture and place into 350-degree oven for about 5 minutes to heat the beans. Serve hot with a slice of raw onion on top of each pepper. Additional onion slices may be served on the plate with stuffed peppers.

BARBECUED WAX BEANS

1 can (1 lb.) wax beans with liquid	2 onions, sliced
1 teaspoon salt	1 tablespoon flour
Pepper to taste	2 tablespoons brown sugar
Cayenne to taste	1/4 teaspoon dry mustard
4 slices white fatback	Salt and pepper to taste
1 apple, peeled and sliced	2 tablespoons apple cider vinegar
Love	Patience

Heat in a saucepan over medium heat the wax beans with liquid from can, salt, pepper, and cayenne until blended. Drain beans, reserving 1 cup liquid. Cook the slices of fatback in a heavy skillet until fat is rendered from meat; then remove meat. Add to the fat the apple and onions. Fry until tender, but not brown. Remove apple and onion slices and keep warm. Combine and stir quickly into the hot fat, flour, brown sugar, dry mustard, and salt and pepper to taste. Continue cooking until slightly thickened and add the 1 cup bean liquid and apple vinegar. Add drained beans and cook until thoroughly blended and heated, stirring constantly. Serve on a platter with onion and apple rings as a bed for the barbecued wax beans. Or, apple and onion rings may be used for garnish. Makes 4–5 servings.

And to godliness brotherly kindness; and to brotherly kindness charity.
2 Peter 1:7

Most of us measure our success by what we are able to get. Real success is measured by what we are able to give.

129

WESTERN BEAN SIMMER

3 pounds (8 cups) small pink beans
6 quarts meat stock or canned beef bouillon
1 medium-sized ham bone
1 pound bacon, sliced
8 cloves garlic, minced or mashed
¾ cup onion, finely chopped
3 cups mushrooms, diced
3 pounds lean chuck, ground
1 package (1 lb.) link sausages
Love
6 cups solid pack canned tomatoes, broken up
2 cans (6 oz. each) tomato paste
2 cans (8 oz. each) Spanish-style tomato sauce
1½ teaspoons oregano
6 teaspoons salt, or to taste
3 teaspoons M.S.G. powder
2 teaspoons ground cumin seed
2 tablespoons chile con carne seasoning
3 tablespoons flour
Patience

Wash and pick over beans, put in large kettle, cover with water, and soak overnight. Next morning, pour off water; add meat stock or bouillon and the ham bone. Add more water, if necessary, so beans are fully covered. Cook, covered, about 2 hours. Then remove ham bone and prepare the other ingredients as follows:

Dice bacon, fry until crisp, and add to beans. Fry garlic, onion, and mushrooms in bacon fat until onion becomes golden brown; then add all to beans. Form ground meat into large thick patties or squares and slowly barbecue over charcoal until done; also barbecue sausages.

Break beef into bite-sized pieces and cut sausages into ½-inch slices; add both to beans. Stir in all remaining ingredients except flour. Simmer until beans are almost tender (normally after about 3 to 4 hours total cooking time); taste and add more salt and chile con carne seasoning as desired. Remove small amount of liquid and mix flour into it as you do when making gravy. Add flour mixture and simmer for a final 30 minutes. Makes 20 or more servings.

BEETS AND ONIONS, HARVARD STYLE

⅓ cup sugar
½ teaspoon salt
1 tablespoon cornstarch
½ cup vinegar
2 tablespoons butter

1 teaspoon minced onion
2 small onions, sliced thinly
2 cups sliced beets, cooked
Love
Patience

Combine sugar, salt, cornstarch, and vinegar and cook over very low heat until smooth and thickened, stirring constantly. Keeping pan on very low heat, add butter and minced onion and mix well. Separately, heat the sliced onions and sliced beets until hot and then carefully add to the Harvard sauce mixture. Heat together for 20 minutes. Serves 6.

SHREDDED BEETS

1 can (1 lb.) beets
Butter
Salt to taste

Pepper to taste
Dash of sugar
Love
Patience

He asked water, and she gave him milk; she brought forth butter in a lordly dish.
Judg. 5:25

Shred beets on medium section of shredder. Place shredded beets in a saucepan with a generous amount of butter. Heat thoroughly; then reduce heat and simmer beets. Add salt, pepper, and sugar. Total cooking time is 10–15 minutes. Serve hot. More butter may be added to keep beets moist. Serves 4.

131

BROCCOLI NEW ORLEANS

2 packages frozen broccoli
spears
2 lemons, cored, cut into
julienne strips

2 tablespoons butter
Salt to taste
2 hard-boiled eggs
Love
Patience

Cook broccoli according to instructions on the package, adding several julienne strips of lemon to the water in which broccoli is cooked. Drain. Serve broccoli garnished with the remainder of the fresh lemon strips. Dot generously with butter. Place sliced hard-boiled eggs on top and center of broccoli spears. Salt to taste.

CHEESE HOLLANDAISE ON BROCCOLI

2 packages frozen broccoli
spears
2 eggs
1 large package (8 oz.)
cream cheese

2½ tablespoons lemon
juice
Dash salt
Love
Patience

132

Cook broccoli according to package instructions. Add the eggs, one at a time, to the cream cheese, blending thoroughly after each addition. Add the lemon juice and salt. Place cream cheese mixture into top of a double boiler over hot water, not boiling. Cook, stirring constantly, until the sauce is thick and fluffy. Serve on broccoli.

HERBED BRUSSELS SPROUTS

2 packages frozen Brussels
   sprouts
1 small onion, chopped
1 bay leaf
Love

2 whole cloves
Salt to taste
Dash black pepper
¼ cup butter
Patience

Place Brussels sprouts, onion, bay leaf, cloves, and black pepper in a saucepan with one cup of water salted to taste. Bring to a boil. Reduce heat and simmer for 10 minutes, or until Brussels sprouts are tender. Drain; remove cloves and bay leaf. Melt butter in a skillet and add herbed Brussels sprouts. Cook over low heat, gently stirring so as not to break the sprouts. When delicately browned, they are ready to serve. Makes 6–8 servings.

And Jesus said unto them, Because of your unbelief: for verily I say unto you, If ye have faith as a grain of mustard seed, ye shall say unto this mountain, Remove hence to yonder place; and it shall remove; and nothing shall be impossible unto you. Matt. 17:20

Most of us feel that we are destined to accomplish something great, if someone will just remove the obstacle in our path.

IMPERIAL BRUSSELS SPROUTS

2 packages frozen Brussels
   sprouts
2 cups heavy cream

1 cup Parmesan cheese
Love
Patience

Cook the Brussels sprouts until tender; drain away cooking water. To prepare Imperial Sauce, place 2 cups of heavy cream into a double boiler. Stir in 1 cup of Parmesan cheese. Heat through. To serve, put Brussels sprouts on a platter and pour the Imperial Sauce over top.

133

CABBAGE AND BRUSSELS SPROUTS ORIENTAL

¼ cup butter
1 small head cabbage, coarsely shredded
1 can water chestnuts, thinly sliced
1 package frozen Brussels sprouts
1 package (3 oz.) cream cheese
Love

¼ cup milk
Dash of garlic salt
½ teaspoon Worcestershire powder
¼ teaspoon soy sauce
Salt to taste
Pepper to taste
Paprika
¼ cup canned chow mein noodles
Patience

Melt butter in a skillet. Add coarsely shredded cabbage and sliced water chestnuts. Sauté cabbage and water chestnuts over low heat for 5 minutes or until cabbage is tender-crisp. Cook Brussels sprouts according to directions on package. Arrange cabbage on serving dish. Drain Brussels sprouts and add to cabbage. Prepare sauce by heating cream cheese, milk, and seasonings together until smoothly blended. Pour the sauce over the Brussels sprouts and top with chow mein noodles.

HOLIDAY CABBAGE

134

4 cups cooked and drained shredded cabbage
2 cups White Sauce
1¼ cups grated Cheddar cheese

2 cups fine bread crumbs
4 tablespoons butter
Salt and pepper to taste
Love
Patience

Combine cabbage, White Sauce, and 1 cup of cheese. Season with salt and pepper to taste and pour into a greased 1½-quart baking dish. Sauté bread crumbs in 4 tablespoons butter. Top cabbage with bread crumbs and then ¼ cup cheese. Bake in a preheated oven at 350 degrees for 25 minutes. Serves 6.

WHITE SAUCE:

2 tablespoons butter	½ teaspoon salt
1½ tablespoons flour	1 cup heated milk

Heat butter in a saucepan or skillet and blend in flour. When mixture is smooth, add salt and heated milk. Over low heat, stir until smooth.

ISLAND CABBAGE

½ medium-sized head of cabbage	½ teaspoon salt
2 tablespoons butter	¼ teaspoon pepper
2 tablespoons sugar	½ cup frozen orange juice concentrate
Juice of ½ lemon	Love
	Patience

Shred cabbage coarsely (this will make about 3 cups). Melt the butter in a heavy frying pan (8–9-inch size). Add the sugar, lemon juice, salt, pepper, and then the shredded cabbage. Mix together well by stirring for 2 to 3 minutes. Add orange juice concentrate. Simmer slowly over low heat until cabbage is just wilted, stirring occasionally. (Do not overcook cabbage—cook only until thickest portions are barely tender.) Serves 4.

INDIAN CABBAGE

1 medium-sized head cab-
  bage
Salted cold water
3 tablespoons butter
1 tablespoon cumin seed
½ cup buttermilk

1 tablespoon lemon juice
1 tablespoon crushed mint
  leaves
Salt
Dash chili pepper
Love
Patience

Cut cabbage into julienne strips ¼-inch wide. Soak in salted cold water for 20 minutes. Drain and dry thoroughly. Melt butter in large saucepan over low heat. Add cabbage strips and cumin seed and cook for 10 minutes, stirring occasionally. Add remaining ingredients and continue cooking, stirring constantly, until cabbage is slightly glazed. Serve at once. Makes 8 servings.

RED CABBAGE DOVER

5 cups shredded red cab-
  bage (1 head)
2 cups water
1 teaspoon salt
4 slices bacon, diced
2 teaspoons brown sugar
Love

2 teaspoons flour
½ cup water
⅓ cup vinegar
1 teaspoon salt
⅛ teaspoon pepper
1 small onion, sliced
Patience

Cook cabbage in 2 cups salted water (1 teaspoon salt) in covered pan 5 to 8 minutes, or until crisp-tender. Drain. Fry bacon; remove bacon and half of bacon fat. Add sugar and flour to remaining fat; blend and add ½ cup water, vinegar, salt, pepper, and onion. Cook until thick, about 5 minutes. Add part of bacon and cabbage; heat through. Garnish with rest of diced bacon. Serves 6.

FRESH BUTTERED CARROTS

12 young, tender carrots	Salt to taste
¼ cup butter	1 teaspoon sugar
Love	Patience

Wash, peel, and cut the carrots in half. Cover with water and boil about 10 minutes, or until carrots are tender. Drain. Add butter, salt, and sugar. Gently toss carrots around in the seasonings. Cook about 5–10 minutes or until liquid cooks down and thickens a little. Serve hot. Serves 4.

SWEET CARROT BAKE

Who can understand his errors? cleanse thou me from secret faults. Ps. 19:12

8 carrots, shredded	Dash salt
2 cups water	½ cup salad oil
3 tablespoons flour	3 tablespoons raisins
3 tablespoons sugar	2 tablespoons butter
Love	Patience

Evil men excuse their faults as being human. Righteous men strive for improvement.

Shred carrots and boil in 1 cup of water until tender. In a separate container, mix flour, sugar, salt, and another 1 cup of water; stir until thoroughly dissolved. Then add to the carrots. Add salad oil to carrot mixture and place in small covered pan. Cook slowly for about 20 minutes. Turn carrot mixture into a small lightly greased baking dish. Sauté the raisins in butter and mix most of them into the carrot mixture. Sprinkle the rest on top. Bake in a slow oven, 250 degrees, for about 20 minutes, or until lightly brown.

137

CAULIFLOWER WITH CHEESE SAUCE

1 large head of cauliflower, or 2 medium-sized ones	Dash of M.S.G. powder
Juice of ½ lemon	Love
2 teaspoons salt	Patience

Cut off tough end of stem and large leaves of the head of cauliflower, leaving on a few green, tender leaves. Place, head up, in 1 inch of boiling water in uncovered saucepan. Add the lemon juice, salt, and M.S.G. powder. Reduce heat to simmer and cook until tender—about 15 minutes. Remove from heat. Drain. Arrange cauliflower in serving dish. Pour the Cheese Sauce from the following recipe over cauliflower.

CHEESE SAUCE:

2 tablespoons butter	¾ cup milk
2 tablespoons flour	1½ cups grated sharp American cheese

Melt butter in a saucepan. Add flour, stirring until smooth. Slowly add milk. Cook until smooth and thickened. Stir in grated cheese until melted. Makes one cup.

CAULIFLOWERETS WITH CAPERS

2 packages frozen cauliflower, broken into flowerettes	1 cup vinegar
	1 cup oil
	1 small bottle of capers, or
Salt and pepper to taste	(⅓ cup)
Love	Patience

Cook cauliflower according to directions on package. Add salt and pepper to taste. When cooked, drain thoroughly. Pour mixture of vinegar and oil over cauliflower and toss around well. After mixing, drain off any extra liquid. Chill. When ready to serve, add the capers and toss together once more, gently. Salt and pepper to taste once more.

If desired, serve with The New French Dressing, p. 53.

BRAISED CELERY AND TOMATOES

2 tablespoons butter
2 cups celery, 1-inch pieces
¼ teaspoon salt
⅛ teaspoon pepper
Love

¼ teaspoon onion salt
2 cups quartered, peeled
   tomatoes, or 1 can (1 lb.)
   tomatoes
Patience

Melt butter in a saucepan or small skillet with a tight cover. Add celery, salt, pepper, and onion salt. Simmer, covered, about 10–15 minutes, or until tender-crisp. Add tomatoes. Cook 5 minutes longer, covered. Celery should be tender and tomatoes should be hot when ready to serve. Makes 4 servings.

CELERY AU GRATIN

2 cups sliced celery
2 tablespoons butter
2 tablespoons flour
½ cup milk
Love

¼ cup grated Cheddar
   cheese
2 tablespoons crushed corn
   chips
Patience

139

In saucepan containing ½ inch water, cook celery over low heat until tender. Drain, reserving liquid. Melt butter in saucepan. Stir in flour and continue to cook while gradually stirring in milk and ¼ cup liquid reserved from celery. Stir mixture occasionally until thick. Add grated cheese. Put celery into greased 1-quart baking dish, add sauce, and top with crushed corn chips. Bake in moderate 350-degree oven for about 15 minutes until thoroughly heated.

CELERY MADRID

½ cup chopped onion
½ cup chopped green pep-
  per
2 tablespoons butter
Love

2½ cups cooked tomatoes
  (about six medium-sized
  tomatoes)
2 cups diced celery
1 teaspoon salt
Patience

Sauté onion and green pepper in butter for about 5 minutes. Add cooked tomatoes (not canned), celery, and salt. Cover and cook over low heat for 25 minutes until celery is tender. Serves 6.

CELERY ORIENTAL

6–8 large stalks of celery
  (outside stalks)
Water
Salt to taste
3 tablespoons butter

1 cup mushroom pieces,
  fresh if available
¼ cup toasted almond
  halves
Love
Patience

Cut celery stalks in thin, diagonal slices. Cook in boiling salted water until barely done, but still crisp. In the butter sauté the mushrooms. Add celery slices and toasted almond halves. Stir well until all ingredients are mixed and heated through. Serves 6.

ANGEL CORN

2 cups cooked fresh corn, cut from cob
1 cup heavy cream
Dash of nutmeg
Salt to taste
Pepper to taste

3 tablespoons melted butter
3 eggs, separated
4 tablespoons grated Swiss cheese
Love
Patience

Blend cooked corn, heavy cream, nutmeg, salt and pepper, melted butter, and beaten egg yolks. Fold in stiffly beaten egg whites and turn into buttered baking dish. Top with grated cheese and place into preheated oven at 300 degrees. Bake for 30 minutes. Increase oven to 375 degrees and brown top of the recipe for about 10 minutes. Serves 4.

At that time Jesus went on the sabbath day through the corn: and his disciples were a hungered, and began to pluck the ears of corn, and to eat.
Matt. 12:1

CORN ON THE COB

Use either 3 to 4 packages frozen corn on the cob, or 8 to 10 ears fresh corn.

Boil the corn in water seasoned to taste with salt. When ready for serving, place corn in a bucket to keep it warm, or wrap each ear in aluminum foil to retain heat. For children, if they like corn buttered, it is a good idea to butter it at the stove or in the kitchen *before* it is served.

141

CORN PUDDING

¼ cup chopped green pepper
1 tablespoon butter
1 tablespoon flour
½ teaspoon sugar
1 cup milk, scalded

2 teaspoons salt
⅛ teaspoon pepper
4 eggs, slightly beaten
2 cups cream-style canned corn
Love
Patience

Sauté the green pepper in butter and blend in the flour. Mix the sugar, milk, salt, and pepper into the slightly beaten eggs. Then stir in the cream-style corn, mixing thoroughly. Pour into a greased 6-cup casserole. Bake in moderately slow oven, 325 degrees, for 1 hour or until set. Serves 6.

LUAU CORN

142

Several ears of fresh corn (frozen corn may be used)
Green onion, finely minced
Chopped bacon
Love

Sour cream
Pats of butter
Salt and pepper to taste
1 loaf French or sourdough bread
Patience

Place each ear of shucked corn on a sheet of aluminum foil. Sprinkle one tablespoon of finely minced green onion over each ear of corn. Then top corn with one tablespoon of chopped bacon. Lightly coat each ear of corn with sour cream and add a pat of butter. Salt and pepper to taste, and then securely wrap the foil enclosing the seasoned ear of corn. Bake for 20 minutes over hot coals, or in the oven at 400 degrees for 30 minutes. Be sure to turn the corn several times during the cooking process.

Serve in large loaf of French or sourdough bread, warmed. To prepare bread, cut bread loaf down the middle with a bread knife. Wedge the center open and scoop out crumbs and loose pieces. Place the already cooked corn in the middle of the bread and serve Hawaiian style.

They that dwell under his shadow shall return; they shall revive as the corn, and grow as the vine: the scent thereof shall be as the wine of Lebanon.
Hos. 14:7

TERERO CORN

3 cups whole kernel corn, drained
1 teaspoon paprika
1 tablespoon chili powder
1 tablespoon Worcestershire powder
Dash Tabasco
Salt and pepper to taste
Love

1 lb. Cheddar cheese, grated
2 cans tamales, cut into small pieces
1 cup ripe olives, cut into small pieces
½ cup (1 stick) butter or margarine
1 cup fine bread crumbs
Patience

Mix together drained corn, paprika, chili powder, Worcestershire powder, and Tabasco. Add salt and pepper to taste. Divide corn, cheese, tamales, olives, and butter into thirds. Line a buttered baking dish with a layer of corn, then cheese, tamales, olives, and then dot with butter. Repeat until all ingredients except bread crumbs are used. Top with bread crumbs. Place baking dish into a preheated 350-degree oven and bake for 30 minutes.

143

PIMIENTO CHEESE CORN CUPS

½ lb. Cheddar cheese
1 can (2 oz.) pimientos
1 can (17 oz.) whole kernel corn
Love

2 teaspoons butter
Salt to taste
Pepper to taste
6 green peppers
Patience

Dice cheese and pimientos into small pieces and mix with corn. Add butter and salt and pepper to taste. Cut tops from green peppers, removing about ¼ inch from each pepper. Core out peppers and stuff with the corn and pimiento mixture. Preheat oven to 400 degrees. Place stuffed peppers into uncovered greased baking dish and bake for 30 minutes, or until cheese is thoroughly melted.

EGGPLANT AU GRATIN, STUFFED

1 large eggplant
½ cup water
½ teaspoon salt
1 tablespoon butter
¼ cup chopped onion
1 tablespoon chopped parsley
1 can (10¾ oz.) condensed cream of mushroom soup

1 teaspoon Worcestershire powder
1 cup fine round cracker crumbs (about 24)
1 tablespoon butter
1 cup mild Cheddar cheese, grated
1½ cups water
Love
Patience

144

Slice off one side of the eggplant and remove pulp from both pieces to within a half inch of the skin. Heat water and salt to boiling, and cook eggplant pulp in the salted water until tender—about 10 minutes. Drain well. Melt butter and cook onion in it until tender, but not brown. Add eggplant pulp, parsley, mushroom soup, Worcestershire powder, and all of the cracker crumbs. Fill egg-plant shell with mixture and place into a 10 x 6 x 2-inch baking dish. Dot with butter and sprinkle the Cheddar cheese on top.

Pour 1½ cups water very carefully into the bottom of the baking dish. Bake in a 375-degree oven for 1 hour or until heated through to center of eggplant. Serves 4–6.

ITALIAN EGGPLANT

2 medium-sized, heavy eggplants
½ medium-sized onion,
  chopped
Olive oil or butter
1 lb. ground meat
Salt and pepper to taste

Garlic salt to taste
1 egg
Crushed cracker crumbs
Butter
Love
Patience

Awake, O north wind; and come, thou south; blow upon my garden, that the spices thereof may flow out. Let my beloved come into his garden, and eat his pleasant fruits.
Song of Sol. 4:16

Cut eggplants in half. Place the halves in a kettle and cover with water; add a little salt and allow to boil until pulp is tender. Remove the eggplant halves from the water. Being careful not to damage the shells, remove the pulp from each shell, leaving clean shells. Place pulp in a bowl and allow to cool.

Sauté onion in a skillet in hot olive oil or butter. When onion is soft, add ground meat and cook until well done. Finely chop the eggplant pulp. Combine pulp with the meat and season with salt, pepper, and garlic salt to taste. Then add egg and mix together thoroughly.

Place the eggplant shells in a greased baking dish and fill each one with the meat mixture. Cover filled shells generously with crushed cracker crumbs. Dot with pats of butter. Place in preheated 400-degree oven and heat through, allowing tops to brown.

145

CREAM OF HOMINY CASSEROLE

1 large onion, minced
1 tablespoon butter
3 cans (15 oz. each)
  hominy
½ can condensed cream of
  mushroom soup
1 can (10¾ oz.) cream of
  celery soup
1 large can Parmesan
  cheese

1 tablespoon Worcester-
  shire powder
Juice of 1 lemon
1 small jar (2 oz.) pi-
  miento, minced
Salt and pepper to taste
Paprika to taste
Bread crumbs
Love
Patience

Sauté onion in butter. Add hominy, heat through. Add mushroom soup and celery soup. Blend in Parmesan cheese, Worcestershire powder, lemon juice, and minced pimiento. Season with pepper, paprika, and salt. Place mixture in a casserole dish and cover with bread crumbs. Bake 45 minutes in a 350-degree oven. Garnish with pimiento pieces. Serves 4.

HOMINY CHEESE RING

1 cup milk
1 tablespoon butter
2 eggs, beaten
1 teaspoon salt
Love

¼ teaspoon paprika
2 cups canned (1 lb. can)
  white hominy, drained
½ cup grated Cheddar
  cheese
Patience

Combine the milk, butter, beaten eggs, salt, and paprika with the hominy. Mix together well. Add the grated cheese and mix well. Place the whole mixture into a greased ring mold (4-cup size) and bake in a moderate oven, 350 degrees. Cook until firm, for about 25 minutes. Remove hominy and cheese ring from the mold, turning out onto a serving plate. The center may be filled with greenery such as lettuce leaves, celery tops, olives, or green pepper rings. Makes 4 servings.

PLANTATION OKRA

1 cup cut okra
6 bacon slices
1 medium onion, chopped
1 green pepper, chopped
1 tablespoon sugar
1 teaspoon flour
Love

½ teaspoon salt
½ teaspoon pepper
1 cup canned stewed toma-
    toes, drained
Whole okra for garnish
Tiny cocktail onions, gar-
    nish
Patience

Cook okra in salted water. Boil for 10 minutes. Drain. Fry bacon and remove slices from skillet but retain for garnish. In bacon grease, brown onion and green pepper. Add seasonings, flour, and stewed tomatoes. Stir. Add okra and continue cooking on low heat. When vegetables are tender, serve with garnishes of whole okra, onions, and bacon slices. Serves 4.

A man's heart deviseth his way: but the Lord directeth his steps.
Prov. 16:9

Life is like a staircase; each step takes us either up or down. Many of us never reach the top as we are reluctant to leave the crowd at the bottom.

SAUTÉED ONION SLICES

12 medium-sized onions
¼ cup butter
Love

Salt
Soy sauce
Patience

147

Slice onions ¼ inch thick. In hot butter in large skillet, sauté onions slowly, turning often, 25 to 30 minutes, or until tender and golden. Sprinkle with salt and soy sauce to taste. Makes 6 servings.

CHILI STUFFED ONIONS

½ cup diced green pepper
½ tablespoon salad oil
2 cans (19 oz. each) chili,
  without beans
6 large onions, peeled
2 eggs, beaten
Love

¼ teaspoon salt
½ teaspoon pepper
2 tablespoons flour
¼ cup raw onion slivers
6 tablespoons grated
  cheese
Patience

Sauté the diced green peppers in salad oil until soft; add to the chili mixture and simmer over low heat. Boil six onions until barely tender. Scoop out centers of the cooked onions. Beat eggs, and blend in salt, pepper, and flour. Dip the onions into the egg mixture and deep-fat-fry until golden brown. Ladle chili mixture into the centers of the fried onions and sprinkle with raw onion slivers. Top each with 1 tablespoon of grated cheese. Serve hot.

ONIONS AND BACON

24 small onions, peeled
1 tablespoon vinegar
¼ lb. bacon, cut into small
  pieces
Love

1 teaspoon salt
¼ teaspoon cracked black
  pepper
Paprika
Patience

148

Put the onions in a kettle with water to cover. Add vinegar, bacon, salt and pepper. Cook these ingredients uncovered until the onions are soft and tender and the liquid has almost cooked away. Sprinkle with paprika for serving. Serves 6.

ONIONS WISCONSIN

6–8 large white onions
1 cup water
2 large packages (8 oz.
  each) cream cheese
Love

2 tablespoons butter
Milk, about ¼ cup
½ cup fresh chives,
  chopped
Patience

Clean outer skin and cut ends from large white onions. Place in a buttered dish with one cup of water. Cover dish and place into oven that has been preheated for 10 minutes at 400 degrees. Bake for 30 minutes or until onions are tender. Remove from oven and serve in bowl or on platter. Over the onions pour cheese sauce made in the following manner:

Place cream cheese, butter, and milk into a double boiler over hot water. When cheese, butter, and milk have melted and blended together, pour over the onions. As onions are served, sprinkle chopped, fresh chives over each one.

FRENCH STYLE PEAS

10 lettuce leaves
3 cups canned green peas
½ teaspoon salt
Love

Dash pepper
Dash nutmeg
1 teaspoon sugar
¼ cup butter
Patience

Wash lettuce leaves. Line bottom and sides of heavy saucepan with leaves. Add peas, salt, pepper, nutmeg, and sugar. Gently mix. Add butter. Cover peas with more lettuce leaves and cook in a covered saucepan over low heat about 25 minutes. Discard lettuce leaves. Serve on small platter or bowl. Serves 6.

149

CREAMY PEAS IN PATTY SHELLS

1 package frozen ready-to-bake patty shells
1 can (17 oz.) English green peas with liquid
2 tablespoons minced onion
½ cup heavy cream
Love

½ can (10¾-oz. size) condensed cream of mushroom soup
Salt to taste
Pepper to taste
Minced parsley
Patience

Bake patty shells according to directions, extra crisp. Heat peas in a saucepan with liquid. Drain. In saucepan blend together onion, cream, mushroom soup, salt, pepper, and parsley and heat through. Spoon hot peas into patty shells. Arrange filled patty shells on a plate. Pour sauce into center of serving plate and over part of the shells. Serves 4–6.

HOPPING JOHN

½ lb. salt pork
1 onion, finely diced
1 can (3 oz.) sliced mushrooms
½ medium-sized green pepper, finely chopped
1½ cups canned tomatoes
Love

1 tablespoon apple cider vinegar
Salt to taste
Pepper to taste
3 cups canned black-eyed peas
3 cups cooked rice
Patience

150

Brown salt pork in a large skillet, rendering as much fat as possible. Remove the pork from the skillet and in the fat sauté the onion, mushrooms, and green pepper. When these ingredients are soft, add the tomatoes, vinegar, and salt and pepper to taste. Simmer this mixture for 3 minutes. Then add the black-eyed peas, rice, and the cooked salt pork that has been sliced. Simmer for a few minutes, just long enough to heat through. Serves 6.

PAPER CUP FRENCH FRIES

3 or 4 packages of frozen French fried potatoes	Salt
Cooking oil	Paper cups, large
Love	Catsup
	Patience

Following directions on the package, deep-fry potatoes in cooking oil. When French fries turn a golden brown, remove them from the cooking oil and drain on paper towels. Salt to taste and place several French fries in each paper cup. Top with catsup for color and extra good taste.

And he took butter, and milk, and the calf which he had dressed, and set it before them; and he stood by them under the tree, and they did eat.
Gen. 18:8

BUTTER-MEG POTATOES

4 potatoes	1½ cups light cream
½ to 1 teaspoon salt	2 tablespoons butter
Pepper generously, but to taste	Nutmeg
Love	Patience

151

Peel potatoes and slice very, very thin. Lightly grease a shallow baking dish, and place the potatoes in it by lay-

152

ers, sprinkling with salt and pepper to taste on each layer. Pour cream over the potatoes until cream covers top layer. Dot with butter and a few dashes of nutmeg.

Bake in a slow oven (275 to 300 degrees). This recipe should cook long enough to absorb all the cream, which will take about 1½ hours. Add more cream if it cooks away before potatoes are done. When done they should be crisp and brown.

BAKED RUSSETS
WITH CHEESE AND BACON

6 large russet potatoes
Salt and pepper to taste
Butter to taste
6 slices American cheese
Love

¼ lb. bacon, fried, drained, and broken into pieces
Paprika
Patience

Bake potatoes in preheated 375-degree oven for approximately 1 hour, or until done. Slightly slit potatoes lengthwise and then again crosswise. Then holding both ends of each potato (with hot pads), gently squeeze together until center of potato breaks into chunky pieces. Salt, pepper, and butter to taste. Return to baking pan and top each potato with a cheese slice, bacon pieces, and paprika. Press center of cheese slice into potato with a large spoon and place potatoes under broiler or back into the oven for 5–10 minutes until cheese begins to melt. Serve hot. Serves 6.

WHIPPED POTATOES

2 lbs. potatoes	½ cup milk, heated
1¼ teaspoons salt	4 tablespoons butter
Enough water to cover	Pepper to taste
Love	Patience

Peel potatoes, half them and quarter each half. Place in saucepan with enough water to cover and 1¼ teaspoons salt. Boil, covered, for 30–35 minutes. Start at high heat and gradually reduce to low heat. When done, drain potatoes and beat with electric beater, or vigorously with potato masher. Add hot milk, butter and return to heat a few minutes. Beat over heat. This makes them fluffier. Serve hot with Brown Gravy. Makes 6 servings.

BROWN GRAVY:

Canned beef gravy may be used and is delicious. If you prefer to make your own, try this recipe.

¼ cup of fat drippings from steak	1 teaspoon gravy seasoning
	Salt to taste
¼ cup flour	Pepper to taste
2 cups warm water (or vegetable liquids)	

Place the fat drippings in a skillet or pan and add flour. Stirring constantly, add the water or vegetable liquids. Simmer and stir until smoothly blended. Add gravy seasoning and stir in thoroughly. Season to taste with salt and pepper. If lumps form in spite of your effort to keep gravy smooth, strain. Pour over potatoes while both are hot and serve at once.

153

DOWN EAST POTATOES

4 to 6 baking potatoes
2 tablespoons butter
8 to 12 tablespoons Cheddar cheese, grated
Salt

Pepper
2 bacon slices, cooked and crumbled into pieces
Love
Patience

Scrub potatoes and bake in a 350-degree oven for 45 minutes. Then slit potatoes about 2½ to 3 inches on one side and remove potato pulp. Place pulp on a plate and mash with fork. Add butter and half the cheese, retaining the rest for topping. Salt and pepper to taste. Crumble crisp pieces of bacon into the potato mixture, retaining a few pieces for topping. Return potato mixture to potato shells. (Ceramic potato shells may be substituted.) Top each potato with more cheese and bacon pieces. Return to oven a few minutes to melt the cheese.

HONEY ALMOND SWEET POTATO WHIP

4 pounds sweet potatoes
4 tablespoons cream
4 tablespoons butter
4 tablespoons honey, and piece of honeycomb
Salt to taste

Dash of ground nutmeg
4 tablespoons slivered almonds
Love
Patience

Cook sweet potatoes in boiling water until tender; peel and mash. Beat, gradually adding cream to make soft and fluffy. Beat in 4 tablespoons butter and 4 tablespoons honey (without honeycomb). Season to taste with salt and ground nutmeg. Serve warm. Place honeycomb on top of whipped sweet potatoes and sprinkle with slivered almonds.

And it came to pass, that on the morrow Moses went into the tabernacle of witness; and, behold, the rod of Aaron for the house of Levi was budded, and brought forth buds, and bloomed blossoms, and yielded almonds.
Num. 17:8

154

BAKED SWEET POTATOES

4 or 5 sweet potatoes
Cooking oil
Love

Butter
Half pineapple rings, for
    garnish (optional)
Patience

Clean sweet potatoes and rub skin surfaces with cooking oil. Bake in a 350-degree oven on a rack or in a baking pan. Bake for 45 to 50 minutes or until tender. Remove from oven and slit with a knife an opening at one side about 2 inches long. Squeeze potato together from end to end and place in a foil wrapper to keep hot. Put a large chunk of butter into the opening and garnish with half of a pineapple ring.

TOMATOES 'N' RICE

2 small tomatoes, peeled,
    diced
¾ cup long grain rice
2 green onions, including
    tops, thinly sliced
½ teaspoon sweet basil

½ teaspoon salt
1 teaspoon sugar
1½ cups chicken broth
1 chicken bouillon cube
Love
Patience

Place tomatoes, rice, green onions, sweet basil, salt, and sugar in a lightly greased casserole which has cover. Mix together. Heat chicken broth; place bouillon cube in broth; stir; let dissolve. Pour broth over the tomato and rice mixture. Bake, covered, in a 375-degree oven for 30 to 40 minutes. Stir casserole contents once or twice while cooking. When the rice is tender, the casserole is ready to serve. Makes 4 large or 6 small servings.

RICE SUPREME

1 tablespoon margarine
1 small onion, finely
  chopped
2 green lettuce leaves,
  shredded
⅓ cup sliced mushrooms
1 large tomato, peeled,
  seeded and chopped
Love

¾ cup rice
1½ cups hot chicken broth
¾ teaspoon salt
Dash of pepper
1 pimiento, diced
2 tablespoons raisins,
  sautéed in a little butter
Paprika
Patience

Melt margarine in saucepan and add onion. Cook until
the onion is soft, but not brown. Add the lettuce, mushrooms, tomato, and rice. Mix together and add the hot
chicken broth, salt, and pepper. Bring to a boil. Cover
and cook over low heat for 20 minutes. Remove from
heat and separate the grains of rice by tossing with a
long-tined kitchen fork. Add the pimiento and sautéed
raisins. Toss again and serve sprinkled with paprika and
garnish with extra raisins.

ORANGE-CASHEW RICE BOWL

3 tablespoons butter
⅔ cup diced celery
2 tablespoons finely
  chopped onion
1½ cups water
1 cup frozen orange juice
  concentrate
Love

2 tablespoons grated
  orange rind
1¼ teaspoons salt
1 cup white rice
½ cup cashew nuts
1 orange, sliced
Parsley for garnish
Patience

Melt butter in a saucepan. Add celery and onion. Cook
until onion is soft, but not browned. Add water, orange

juice concentrate, orange rind, and salt. Bring to a boil. Add rice slowly. Cover. Reduce heat and cook for 25–30 minutes. Toast cashew nuts in oven a minute or two to crisp them.

When rice is ready to serve, line the bottom of the serving bowl with orange slices (reserve one end slice of orange for top garnish). Sprinkle half the cashew nuts over orange slices. Now fill the serving bowl with rice mixture. Garnish top with orange slice and sprinkle with other half of cashew nuts. Line the bowl with parsley.

INDO-SPICES	CONDIMENTS	SIDE DISHES
Ginger	Curry powder	Flaked coconut
Cumin	Bay leaves	White raisins
Mustard seed	Crab apples	Dark raisins
Whole cloves	Button mushrooms	Candied fruit
Nutmeg	Snipped parsley	Almonds
Ripe olives	Green olives	

SPANISH RICE

4 slices bacon
1 cup uncooked rice
1 can (6 oz.) button
  mushrooms
½ cup chopped onion
½ cup chopped green
  pepper
Love
Patience

2½ cups (1 29-oz. can)
  tomatoes, cut in pieces
  and drained
1 teaspoon salt
1 teaspoon paprika
½ teaspoon M.S.G.
  powder
½ teaspoon black pepper
1½ cups boiling water

157

Cut strips of bacon into small pieces and sauté in a skillet. When bacon is brown, remove and set aside, leaving fat in the skillet. Place rice, mushrooms, onion, and green pepper into the skillet and cook, stirring until rice is lightly browned. Return the pieces of bacon to the skillet. Add the tomatoes, salt, paprika, M.S.G. powder, and pepper. Blend in the boiling water and turn whole mixture into a greased 2-quart baking dish. Cover and bake in a preheated 350-degree oven for about 50 minutes, or until rice is tender. Remove cover from the baking dish during the last 10 minutes of the baking period. Serves 6.

158

BUTTERED SPINACH

3 tablespoons butter	Salt and pepper to taste
1 tablespoon minced onion	M.S.G. powder, a dash or two
2 packages frozen leaf spinach	Onion rings, raw, for garnish
Water to cover	Pats of butter, for garnish
Love	Patience

Melt butter in a saucepan large enough for 2 packages of leaf spinach. Sauté the minced onion in butter for a few minutes. Add spinach and enough water to cover bottom of pan. Add salt and pepper to taste and a couple of dashes of M.S.G. powder. Stir gently, but well.

To preserve bright green color of spinach, cook un-covered for first 5 minutes. Total cooking time, over low heat, is 10–15 minutes. Serve hot. Garnish with raw onion rings with a large pat of butter in the center of each onion ring. Serves 6.

SPINACH EUROPA

3 pounds fresh spinach
6 bacon slices
½ cup chopped onion
½ teaspoon ground cinna-
  mon
Love

2 tablespoons red wine
  vinegar
1 teaspoon salt
Pepper to taste
Patience

Wash spinach 2 or 3 times. Cut bacon into 1-inch pieces, and sauté with onion in skillet until onion is slightly browned. Remove skillet from heat; add cinnamon, red wine vinegar, salt and pepper.

Cut spinach leaves crosswise into ½-inch strips, and combine with sautéed bacon, onion, and seasonings. Place in greased baking dish, cover, and bake in a moderate 350-degree oven for 30 minutes, or until spinach is tender. Makes 6 servings.

No one has ever gotten into trouble while studying his Bible.

BAKED ACORN SQUASH

2 medium-sized acorn
  squash
4 teaspoons butter
Love

Salt to taste
Pepper to taste
4 tablespoons brown sugar
Patience

Cut squash into halves and remove seeds. Rub cavities generously with softened butter. Sprinkle each with salt and pepper. Top with a tablespoon of brown sugar sprinkled into each of the squash halves. Place squash into a shallow baking dish and cover tightly (aluminum foil may be used). Bake in a moderate oven, 350 degrees, for about 25 minutes. Remove the cover and bake for 20 additional minutes until each squash is tender. Serves 4.

159

SQUASH LOAF

1½ cups frozen yellow squash, cooked and drained	1 onion, diced
¾ cup cracker crumbs	2 eggs, beaten
2 tablespoons butter	¼ lb. grated American cheese
¾ cup milk	Salt to taste
Love	Pepper to taste
	Patience

Mash the cooked and drained squash. Add other ingredients, reserving enough cracker crumbs and cheese for topping. Form into a loaf. Top with crumbs and cheese. Bake in moderate 350-degree oven for 45 minutes. Makes 4 servings.

*And one went out into the field to gather herbs, and found a wild vine, and gathered thereof wild gourds his lap full, and came and shred them into the pot of pottage: for they knew them not.
2 Kings 4:39*

SAUTÉED SQUASH AND ONIONS

4 to 5 tablespoons shortening, melted	1 cup water
2 packages frozen crookneck sliced squash	Salt to taste
	Pepper to taste
2 medium-to-large-sized onions, peeled and sliced	½ cup grated American cheese
Love	Paprika
	Patience

Place the melted shortening in a heavy skillet. Set at a medium temperature. Allow squash to partially thaw and place into shortening. Add onion slices. Sauté squash and onions until they begin to soften, but not brown. Turn two or three times for even sautéeing. Add water and place a lid on the skillet. Let simmer for 15 to 20 minutes. Salt and pepper to taste. Remove squash from skillet to serving dish. While hot, sprinkle with American cheese. Top with paprika. Serves 6.

BAKED ZUCCHINI WITH CHEESE IN SHELLS

1½ lbs. small zucchini
1½ cups water
1½ cups bread crumbs
¾ cup grated process
   American cheese
¼ cup minced onion
1¼ teaspoons salt
Love

2 tablespoons snipped
   parsley
⅛ teaspoon pepper
2 eggs, beaten
3 tablespoons butter
Paprika
Patience

For as the earth bringeth forth her bud, and as the garden causeth the things that are sown in it to spring forth; so the Lord God will cause righteousness and praise to spring forth before all the nations. Isa. 61:11

Wash and scrub zucchini. Snip off ends and cook whole in about 1½ cups of water in covered pan. Boil about 10 minutes. Mix together bread crumbs, ½ cup process American cheese, onion, salt, parsley, pepper, and eggs. Preheat oven to 350 degrees. Cut zucchini into halves lengthwise. Gently scoop out pulp from the shells, and chop into small pieces. Mix with bread crumb mixture.

Spoon zucchini mixture gently into zucchini shells. Dot with butter. Now sprinkle ¼ cup grated cheese over filled zucchini. Sprinkle with paprika. Place shells in a baking pan or dish and bake uncovered for 25–35 minutes. When brown on top, zucchini is ready to serve. Serves 4–6.

BROILED TOMATOES PARMESAN

6 medium-to-large sized
   tomatoes
6 canned button mush-
   rooms, drained
6 teaspoons butter

Parmesan cheese
Paprika
Love
Patience

161

Cut about ¼ of the top of each tomato off. Core out a tiny section in the center and place a button mushroom in each center. Top each tomato with a teaspoon of butter and sprinkle with Parmesan cheese and paprika. Broil for about 10 minutes or until tomato tops are lightly brown.

SCALLOPED TOMATOES

1 cup chopped onion
1 can (1 lb.) tomatoes, drained
½ cup cheese cracker crumbs
1 tablespoon parsley flakes
1½ teaspoons sugar
Love

1 teaspoon seasoned salt
1 cup thick sour cream
2 tablespoons butter
3 slices crisp toast, cut in ¼ to ½-inch cubes
Extra parsley flakes for top
Patience

Grease a shallow 1¼-quart baking dish. Mix the onion, tomatoes, cracker crumbs, and a mixture of parsley flakes, sugar, and seasoned salt in the baking dish. Spoon sour cream evenly over mixture. Heat butter in a skillet. Add toast cubes and toss until sides are coated. Top sour cream with toast cubes. Sprinkle with parsley flakes. Heat thoroughly in a 325-degree oven about 20 minutes. Serve in sauce dishes. Makes 6 servings.

He causeth the grass to grow for the cattle, and herb for the service of man: that he may bring forth food out of the earth: Ps. 104:14

TOMATO CHEESE SCANDIA

4 canned whole tomatoes, well drained
1 cup grated American cheese
⅓ cup thinly sliced onion
Love

½ teaspoon salt
⅛ teaspoon pepper
1 cup bread crumbs (or crushed potato chips)
Paprika
Patience

162

Preheat oven to 350 degrees. Cut tomatoes into chunky pieces. Place half of tomatoes into a greased casserole.

Place cheese and then onion slices, using half of each, on top of the tomatoes. Sprinkle with salt and pepper. Repeat: tomatoes, cheese, onions. Salt and pepper again. Top with bread crumbs, or potato chips, and paprika. Bake for about 30 minutes or until cheese is melted and bubbly hot. Do not cover while baking. Serves 4.

SCALLOPED TURNIPS

3 medium-sized turnips	1 teaspoon salt
2 tablespoons butter	1/8 teaspoon pepper
2 tablespoons flour	1/2 cup grated American
1 1/2 cups milk	cheese
Love	Patience

Peel and slice turnips. Boil them in salted water in a saucepan for about 15 minutes. Meanwhile, make a white sauce with the butter, flour, milk, salt and pepper. When turnips are tender, drain and pour the white sauce over them. Sprinkle grated cheese on top. Bake about 10 minutes in a 350-degree oven. Serve hot. Makes 4 servings.

GARDEN PASTA

Butter	2 cups frozen green peas,
1 cup frozen cut corn,	cooked
cooked	1 can (32 oz.) ravioli and
1 cup frozen lima beans,	sauce
cooked	Love
6 stalks broccoli, fresh or	Patience
frozen, cooked	

163

In a buttered casserole put the corn, lima beans, broccoli with the tough ends cut off, and green peas. Spread contents of a can of ravioli over the vegetables, being careful not to break the pastry cases. Cover all the ingredients with the sauce. Bake in a hot oven, 450 degrees, for 20 minutes or until delicately browned.

VEGETABLE TRIO

1 or 2 packages frozen crookneck squash
1 or 2 packages frozen Brussels sprouts
1 or 2 packages frozen whole okra

Salt and pepper to taste
¼ cup butter, melted
M.S.G. powder
Love
Patience

Cook all the vegetables according to directions on packages. Salt and pepper to taste. Melt ¼ cup butter and add a few dashes of M.S.G. powder to butter. When ready to serve, pour butter generously over vegetables which have been arranged on a platter or in a bowl.

LAZY SUSAN OF VEGETABLES

TOMATOES, SWEDISH:

6 medium-sized tomatoes
Salt
12 oz. fresh spinach, or about ¾ cup, chopped

1 egg yolk
½ cup light cream
3 tablespoons butter

164

Slice off the top of each tomato and core out a little of the center. Salt the inside. Cook spinach a minimum of time until tender. Drain. Combine the egg yolk and cream and add the spinach and butter which has been melted. Bake in a casserole dish at a temperature of 375 degrees for about 15–20 minutes. Serve hot. A dot of additional butter may be added as it is served.

ONIONS, RELISH:

1½ dozen very small, young onions	Pinch sugar
1 cup water	Dash pepper
Salt	2 teaspoons vinegar

Boil onions in water seasoned with salt, sugar, pepper, vinegar. Boil just until tender. Drain. Adjust seasoning with more salt and pepper if desired.

MIDGET BEETS:

1 can midget beets	Salt
Butter	Pepper

Heat beets and drain. Dot generously with butter; season with salt and pepper. Return to heat and gently stir until beets are glazed with butter.

SQUASH STUFFED WITH GREEN PEAS:

8 to 12 yellow squash	Salt
1 package frozen green peas	Pepper
	Butter
Love	Patience

Clean and halve squash. Put into salted boiling water for about 10–15 minutes. Remove squash from water. Scoop out centers. Cook peas according to package directions. Drain and place in center of squash. Salt and pepper and dot with butter.

Only by pride cometh contention: but with the well advised is wisdom. Prov. 13:10

Wisdom is one of the few possessions we can have that cannot be purchased on an easy payment plan.

165

SABZI

1 onion, coarsely chopped	½ teaspoon pepper
2 tablespoons salad oil	¼ teaspoon powdered
2 potatoes, cubed	ginger
2 carrots, diced	¼ teaspoon cumin
1 small cauliflower, bro-	⅛ teaspoon cayenne
ken into clusters	1 teaspoon curry powder
1 medium eggplant,	2 bay leaves, finely
coarsely diced	crumbled
2 tomatoes, cut in wedges	1½ cups of water
1 tablespoon salt	2 tablespoons melted
Love	butter
	Patience

Sauté the onion in salad oil until soft. Add all of the vegetables and stir around in the oil for 5 minutes. Add the seasonings and water. Cover and simmer for 25 to 30 minutes. As soon as vegetables are tender, drain well and serve hot, with butter poured over the Sabzi. Serves 8.

SAVORY NEW POTATOES AND CARROTS WITH CHIVES

2 pounds small young new	2 packages frozen carrots
potatoes	1 teaspoon salt
1 teaspoon salt	2 tablespoons butter
2 tablespoons butter	1 tablespoon chopped
1 tablespoon chopped	chives
chives	Parsley for garnish
Parsley for garnish	Patience
Love	

Cook unpeeled new potatoes in salted water for about 20 minutes. Remove, cool, and peel. Pour 2 tablespoons melted butter and 1 tablespoon chives over potatoes; salt again to taste, and serve hot.

Cook carrots according to the directions on package, adding salt to cooking water. Remove from heat and drain. Pour 2 tablespoons melted butter and 1 tablespoon chives over carrots and serve hot. Garnish with parsley. These two vegetables may be served together in a double serving dish, or separately.

GREEN PEAS AND GREEN LIMAS, ROMA

1 package frozen green peas
1 package frozen green lima beans
6 tablespoons butter
½ teaspoon onion salt
¼ teaspoon M.S.G. powder
¼ teaspoon oregano
Salt to taste
Love

Cracked black pepper to taste
1 small tomato, diced
2 tablespoons finely chopped ripe olives
1 can (2 oz.) pimientos (strips)
1 can (3 oz.) button mushrooms
½ teaspoon sugar
Patience

Don't judge a man for his weakness, for his appetite may be stronger for his temptations than yours.

Cook green peas and green lima beans according to directions on packages; then pour off liquid. Melt butter in a saucepan. Add onion salt, M.S.G. powder, oregano, salt, and cracked black pepper to the butter and mix together. Then add the cooked peas and lima beans and simmer very slowly for 5 minutes, being careful not to scorch them. Add diced tomato, ripe olives, pimientos, mushrooms, and sugar. Simmer, covered, for about 5 minutes longer, stirring gently occasionally. Serve hot. Serves 6–8.

167

VEGETABLE-CHEESE BAKE

4 eggs, separated
1 cup milk
3 slices white bread, crusts removed
¾ teaspoon salt
½ teaspoon dry mustard
¼ teaspoon M.S.G. powder
⅛ teaspoon pepper
1 cup cottage cheese
Love

2 cups finely chopped, cooked vegetables
1 small onion, minced
2 tablespoons minced green pepper or snipped parsley
1 can (10¾ oz.) condensed tomato soup
2 tablespoons butter or margarine
Patience

Day before: In mixing bowl, beat egg yolks with fork. Add milk, bread, salt, mustard, M.S.G., and pepper. Let bread soften; break up with fork. Add cottage cheese, cooked vegetables, onion, and green pepper or parsley. Refrigerate.

About 1 hour before serving: Preheat oven to 350 degrees. Beat egg whites until stiff; fold into vegetable-cheese mixture. Pour into a well-greased 10 x 6 x 2-inch or 8 x 8 x 2-inch baking dish. Bake 45 minutes or until firm. Cut into squares. For sauce, heat soup with butter. Serve squares with hot sauce. Makes 4 servings.

Cheese Dishes

The Lord is my shepherd; I shall not want. He maketh me to lie down in green pastures: he leadeth me beside the still waters. He restoreth my soul: he leadeth me in the paths of righteousness for his name's sake. Yea, though I walk through the valley of the shadow of death, I will fear no evil: for thou art with me; thy rod and thy staff they comfort me. Thou preparest a table before me in the presence of mine enemies: thou anointest my head with oil; my cup runneth over. Surely goodness and mercy shall follow me all the days of my life: and I will dwell in the house of the Lord for ever.

Ps. 23:1–6

If you live today as though it were the last day of your life, there would be no wasted moments. There would be only understanding and tolerance for those with whom you come in contact. There would be only appreciation and love for your family. There would be no time for drunkenness or debauchery. Your work would take on new meaning. Your values would seem entirely different. You would place your life in the hands of the Lord.

CHEESE BALLS

¾ lb. extra-sharp Cheddar
  cheese
3 egg whites
⅓ cup flour
4 dashes Tabasco
Dash salt

1 teaspoon parsley flakes
Paprika
Corn meal
Hot melted shortening or
  oil
Love
Patience

*And honey, and
butter, and
sheep, and
cheese of kine,
for David, and
for the people
that were with
him, to eat: for
they said, The
people is hun-
gry, and weary,
and thirsty, in
the wilderness.*
2 Sam. 17:29

Grate extra-sharp cheddar cheese. Beat egg whites until very stiff. To egg whites, add grated cheese. Then add flour, Tabasco, salt, parsley flakes, and paprika for color. Roll mixture into small balls; then roll balls in corn meal. Place balls in skillet with about ¼-inch hot melted shortening or oil. Allow the cheese balls to cook until golden brown, constantly turning with a long fork. Serve at room temperature.

CHEESE LOG

½ pound sharp Cheddar
  cheese
1 small package (3 oz.)
  cream cheese
1 canned pimiento
1 cup diced roasted al-
  monds

1 tablespoon lemon juice
1 teaspoon salt
1 teaspoon Worcestershire
  powder
1 teaspoon grated onion
Parsley
Love
Patience

Grind together the Cheddar cheese, cream cheese, pimiento, and almonds. Stir in the lemon juice, salt, Worcestershire powder, and onion. Shape into a large roll or loaf on waxed paper. Chill. Serve with pretzels and crackers. Garnish with parsley. Cheese logs may be pre-sliced for serving or individuals may slice as desired.

171

DERBY CHEESE ASSORTMENT

Cheeses for a man's taste. Offer an assortment of Gouda, longhorn, New York sharp, and Cheddar. Serve with selection of crackers.

MACARONI CHEESE BAKE

8 oz. elbow macaroni (about 2 cups)	1 cup commercial sour cream
½ lb. American cheese slices, diced	Buttered bread crumbs
¼ cup butter	Tomato, quartered, for garnish
¾ teaspoon salt	Paprika
¼ teaspoon pepper	Pimiento, for garnish
Love	Patience

Cook elbow macaroni as package instructions direct. Drain. Heat oven to 350 degrees. Using a casserole (1½-quart size), place about ⅓ of the macaroni and ⅓ of the cheese in the bottom, then a little butter dotted here and there, then salt and pepper sprinkled over surface. Add ⅓ of the sour cream. Repeat this pattern until all the ingredients are used. End with sour cream on top and bread crumbs. Bake, covered, for 30 minutes. (If you desire to serve from a chafing dish, bake only 25 minutes and remove baking dish from the oven. Scoop the macaroni and cheese into the chafing dish, decorate top with cheese or bread crumbs, and place chafing pan under the broiler for about five minutes until cheese is melted.) Garnish with tomato quarters, paprika, and a whole pimiento. Serves 5.

SWISS NOODLES

1 pound cottage cheese
¾ cup hot water
2 tablespoons olive oil
3 tablespoons melted
  butter
Love

1 teaspoon salt
½ teaspoon freshly ground
  pepper
1 pound egg noodles
Patience

Hast thou not poured me out as milk, and curdled me like cheese?
Job 10:10

Place cottage cheese, hot water, olive oil, melted butter, salt, and pepper in the top of a double boiler. Beat ingredients together until smooth. Place top of double boiler over hot water and heat. Cook noodles, drain well, and mix with hot sauce. Serve hot. Serves 8.

Breads

*Cast thy bread upon the waters: for thou shalt find it after
many days.*

Eccles. 11:1

*The seeds we plant today will be the harvest of tomorrow.
Carefully explore each opportunity and remember . . . If
a door closes, rejoice, for it may have led to failure. Success
is learning to do one thing better than anyone else in the world.*

PRIZE-WINNING HOMEMADE WHITE BREAD

(Sponge Method)

1½ cups warm water (not hot)
2 tablespoons sugar
1 teaspoon salt
1 tablespoon shortening
1 package active dry yeast
2 cups sifted flour

1 cup milk, scalded
2 tablespoons sugar
1 tablespoon salt
3 tablespoons shortening
4½ cups sifted flour
Love
Patience

If thine enemy be hungry, give him bread to eat; and if he be thirsty, give him water to drink.
Prov. 25:21

In a large mixing bowl place warm water, 2 tablespoons sugar, 1 teaspoon salt, and 1 tablespoon shortening. Mix and cool to lukewarm. Stir in active dry yeast until dissolved. Add 2 cups flour. Beat until smooth. Cover; let rise in warm, draft-free place.

In about one hour it should be light and spongy. Scald 1 cup milk. Stir in 2 tablespoons sugar, 1 tablespoon salt, and 3 tablespoons shortening. Cool to lukewarm. Stir yeast mixture down and stir in lukewarm milk mixture. To this, add 4½ cups sifted flour. Turn dough out on lightly floured board. Knead until smooth and elastic. Place in a greased bowl; brush with shortening. Let rise in warm, draft-free place until doubled in bulk, about 45 minutes. Punch down; turn out on lightly floured board. Divide in half, or thirds. Let rest 15–20 minutes. Shape into loaves and place in greased 9 x 5 x 3-inch bread pans. Brush with shortening. Cover. Let rise in warm, draft-free place until center is slightly higher than edge of pan; about one hour. Bake in a moderate (350–375 degrees) oven for about 50 minutes.

And Jacob vowed a vow, saying, If God will be with me, and will keep me in this way that I go, and will give me bread to eat, and raiment to put on.
Gen. 28:20

177

WHITE BREAD LOAF, SCANDIA

Recipe makes two loaves.
1 cake compressed yeast
1 cup lukewarm water
1 cup milk
2 tablespoons sugar
Love

2 teaspoons salt
2½ tablespoons shorten-
  ing
6 cups sifted flour
Small amount of oil
Patience

Add cake of yeast to lukewarm water and let stand for
about 5 minutes to dissolve. Scald milk. Add sugar, salt,
and shortening to milk. Stir. Cool to lukewarm. Add dissolved yeast to lukewarm milk mixture. Add 3 cups of the
sifted flour and beat. When smooth add 3 more cups of
sifted flour. Stir. When dough forms a large ball and does
not stick to sides of bowl, turn out on a slightly floured
board and knead. Fold dough over and over on itself.
Turn dough half around and knead again. Keep board
floured as dough will pick up some of it. However, use
only what is necessary. You just want to keep the dough
from sticking to the board or your hands. After kneading
about 10 minutes, dough should be smooth and elastic
and should not stick to the board.

Put a very small amount of oil in a large mixing bowl.
Remove excess with paper towel. Place kneaded dough-
ball into the oiled bowl and brush it very lightly with oil.
Cover with saran wrap or waxed paper and place the bowl
in a warm place, making sure it is draft-free. In about 80
minutes the dough should double in size. Punch the
dough down with your hands and form into a ball. Now
divide the dough into two parts, shaping each into an ob-
long loaf-sized ball. Pinch edges together to seal and
place sealed side down in oiled bread pans about 8 x 4 x
3 inches. Cover and let loaves rise in a warm place until
doubled in bulk. This should take about 50 minutes.
Bake in a 350-degree oven for about 50 minutes.

178

FRENCH LOAF WITH PARSLEY BUTTER

1 loaf French bread
Cooking oil
⅓ cup butter
Salt to taste
Pepper to taste
Dash or two M.S.G. powder

Dash or two onion salt
Dash garlic salt (optional)
3–4 tablespoons parsley,
    minced, with a few sprigs
    for garnish
Love
Patience

And it shall come to pass, that every one that is left in thine house shall come and crouch to him for a piece of silver and a morsel of bread, and shall say, Put me, I pray thee, into one of the priests' offices, that I may eat a piece of bread.
1 Sam. 2:36

Place French bread loaf in a 375-degree oven to warm and slightly brown, after brushing the top of the loaf with cooking oil. When crust begins to get crisp, remove loaf from oven and slice through, but do not cut the bottom crust. Melt butter in a saucepan. Add salt, pepper, M.S.G. powder, and onion salt. (Garlic salt, if desired.) Stir and continue to heat over lowest temperature. Mince parsley (snip with kitchen scissors) and add to the butter mixture. Stir. Place French loaf on a tray or platter which has been warmed. While bread is still warm, pour the parsley-butter mixture over top, separating slices here and there to allow parsley-butter to drip down into bread. Garnish with parsley sprigs.

PEPPERED BREAD, GRILLED

2 sticks butter
Large (thick) slices of
    French, sourdough, or
    sandwich bread

Black pepper
Love
Patience

179

Melt butter in large, heavy skillet. Grill one side of bread and then the other, peppering each side generously to taste. Serve warm.

CORN MUFFINS

2 eggs
4 tablespoons sugar
⅔ cup milk
½ cup shortening, melted
Love

1⅓ cups flour
⅔ cup yellow corn meal
3 teaspoons baking powder
½ teaspoon salt
Patience

Beat eggs until light and mix with sugar, milk, and shortening. Sift the flour, corn meal, baking powder, and salt together. Add liquid mixture to the dry mixture all at one time. Blend, using as few strokes as possible. (Do not beat). Fill greased muffin pans about ⅔ full. Bake in a hot, 400-degree oven for 20 minutes. Serve warm. Makes 12 muffins.

FRITTER CORN BREAD

3 egg yolks
1⅔ cups canned whole
  kernel corn, drained
½ teaspoon salt
Pepper to taste
Love

Dash garlic salt
1 tablespoon minced onion
¼ cup sifted flour
3 egg whites, beaten
Salad oil
Patience

180

Beat egg yolks until they are a lemony color; add corn, salt, pepper, garlic salt, onion, and flour. Fold in beaten egg whites. Drop batter from pitcher into hot oil in a heavy skillet. Brown on one side, turn, and brown opposite side.

PECAN-CORN MUFFINS PETITE

½ cup pecans, broken
   pieces
1 package corn muffin mix
Love

Butter
Cherry preserves
Patience

Place pecans on a cookie sheet and toast in a moderate 350-degree oven for about 10 minutes, or until nuts are crisp. (If you are using a large package of muffin mix increase pecan pieces to ¾ cup.) Remove and set aside. Blend corn muffin mix by directions on package. Add the pecans and bake according to directions on package.

Serve with swirls or tiny pats of butter and cherry preserves.

ONION SHORTBREAD

4 tablespoons margarine
6 small onions, thinly
   sliced
1 egg, beaten
1 teaspoon salt
Love

Enough biscuit dough to
   cover 8 x 12-inch flat pan
5 slices bacon, uncooked
Tiny whole onions for
   garnish (optional)
Patience

Melt margarine in a skillet and sauté onions until soft. Remove from heat and blend in beaten egg and salt. Roll out biscuit dough about ½-inch thick onto pan. Over the dough spread the onion and egg mixture and chop up the uncooked bacon in small pieces and sprinkle on top. Bake in a 450-degree oven until brown, approximately 20 minutes. Tiny whole onions may be used for garnish, if desired. Serves 6.

DATE-NUT BREAD

¾ cup chopped walnuts
1 cup cut-up dates, pits removed
1½ teaspoons baking soda
½ teaspoon salt
3˙ tablespoons shortening
1 teaspoon grated lemon rind

¾ cup boiling water
2 eggs
1 teaspoon vanilla extract
1 cup granulated sugar
1½ cups sifted flour
Love
Patience

Combine walnuts, dates, soda, salt, then shortening and lemon rind. Add water and let stand about 30 minutes. Preheat oven to 350 degrees. Prepare one average-sized loaf pan, or two small loaf pans, by greasing. Beat eggs lightly. Add vanilla, sugar, and flour to eggs. Beat together lightly. Blend in date-nut mixture until barely blended. Do not mix too much. Place batter into loaf pan or pans. Bake about 1 hour. Test to see if done. If not you can bake 10 more minutes. Allow bread to cool in the pan for a few minutes. Remove from pan and let loaf cool thoroughly before slicing.

182

BOSTON BROWN BREAD

1 cup water
1½ cups raisins
2 tablespoons shortening
½ cup prune juice
1 egg
1 teaspoon vanilla
1 cup sugar
Love

½ teaspoon salt
2 cups flour
¾ cup wheat germ
2 teaspoons (level) baking soda
½ cup shelled pecans, broken in pieces
Patience

Combine water and raisins and bring to a boil in saucepan. Boil one minute and remove from heat. Blend in shortening. Allow mixture to cool about 10 minutes. Mix in prune juice, egg, and vanilla. Blend thoroughly. Sift together sugar, salt, flour, wheat germ, and baking soda. Exercise caution in measuring baking soda (level measure). Combine these two mixtures and mix, but do not beat. Mix in pecans.

Fill greased baking cans ⅔ full and place into a 350-degree preheated oven. Bake for 45 minutes or longer if necessary until bread is crusty on top. Recipe makes 3 or 4 small loaves depending on the size of baking cans. (Ordinary cans such as those you purchase your vegetables and fruits in may be used.) Clean cans and save best sizes (3½-inch diameter, 6-inch tall) for brown bread baking.

When Jesus then lifted up his eyes, and saw a great company come unto him, he saith unto Philip, Whence shall we buy bread, that these may eat? John 6:5

CONNECTICUT BREAD-NUT STUFFING

(Served as a dressing)

¼ cup margarine, melted	1 tablespoon minced onion
3 cups soft white bread crumbs	1 tablespoon minced parsley
¾ teaspoon salt	½ cup hot water
¼ teaspoon pepper	¾ cup chopped walnuts
2 teaspoons poultry seasoning	Love
	Patience

On low heat in large saucepan combine all ingredients, tossing constantly, and heat until hot. Serve with leg of lamb. Pour just a little of the gravy recipe over the dressing for added flavor and moisture.

183

Desserts

Be kindly affectioned one to another with brotherly love; in honour preferring one another.

Rom. 12:10

The secret of life is to love, not to receive love. To give freely and not to expect to get. To be of service rather than being served. To be a strong light in the dark to another who cannot see. To be a hand of strength to anyone who is weak. Through love we find life.

MINIATURE APPLE DUMPLINGS

BASIC CREAM CHEESE DOUGH:

1 cup flour	4 oz. cream cheese (cold)
½ cup (1 stick) butter	Love
(cold)	Patience

Sift flour into a mixing bowl. Cut butter and cream cheese into the flour with a knife (as for pie crust). Continue cutting in until pieces are the size of peas and each piece of solid is well coated with flour. With your hands, squeeze mixture together over and over until a ball of dough is formed. Chill for several hours. When ready to make apple dumplings, roll out as for pie crust. (Be sure to cover crust well with flour, or egg whites, before placing apples onto crust, to absorb the fruit juices and keep the crust on bottom flaky.) This Basic Cream Cheese Dough should always be baked in a preheated 450-degree oven.

While traveling, we often see signs advertising "Homemade Pies." After tasting the cardboard crust and the starch filling, we wonder what awful homes they come from.

APPLE DUMPLINGS:

12 small apples, sour (if	Flour
large, 6)	Lemon juice
Cinnamon	Sugar

Cut rolled-out dough into about 12 squares. Peel, core, and quarter the apples. (If large apples are used, slice into small wedges.) Onto each square of dough place four quarters of apple. Sprinkle cinnamon, flour, lemon juice, and sugar over and in between the quartered apples. Enclose apples by folding dough like an envelope, overlapping each side and end. Bake in a preheated 450-degree oven until apples are tender, about 30 minutes. Yield: 12 miniature dumplings (or 6 large ones).

APPLE CREAM PIE

Spikenard and saffron; cala- mus and cinna- mon, with all trees of frankin- cense; myrrh and aloes, with all the chief spices. Song of Sol. 4:14

1 10-inch unbaked pastry shell
10 cups quartered pared apples (about 10 large apples, Winesaps or Rome Beauties)
2 cups sugar
4 tablespoons flour
1 teaspoon salt

⅓ cup light cream
¼ cup milk
¼ teaspoon cinnamon
Dash of nutmeg
¼ cup grated Cheddar cheese
Love
Patience

Heap unbaked pie shell with the quartered apples. Combine sugar, flour, and salt; add cream and milk; beat well. Pour over apples. Sprinkle with cinnamon and nutmeg. Bake in moderate (375 degrees) oven 1½ to 2 hours or until apples are soft. (Cover pie loosely with aluminum foil for first hour of baking, then remove foil.) Serve warm with grated Cheddar cheese.

CHERRY COBBLER JUBILEE

1 pie crust mix (bottom and top crust)
1½ cups cherry juice
1 cup sugar
2–3 tablespoons flour
Love

2–3 tablespoons cornstarch
2½ cups canned, pitted sour cherries
2 tablespoons butter
1 tablespoon lemon juice
Patience

Prepare pastry according to package instructions and line a square pyrex baking dish, saving enough pastry for top crust. Saving juice, drain cherries. Add sugar to cherry juice and bring to boil. Add flour and cornstarch. Cook until mixture thickens. Add cherries and remove from heat. Add butter and lemon juice. Pour filling into pastry-lined baking dish. Apply top crust. Brush top crust (not the edges) with a little milk. Preheat oven 10 minutes at 375 degrees. Bake pie for 30 minutes or longer until crust is brown. Remove from oven and allow to cool, in order to thicken the cherry juice.

There are more Gourmesses in the kitchen than Gourmets.

GRAPEFRUIT PIE

3 tablespoons red hots (Cinnamon Imperials)
1 cup juice from canned grapefruit
1 cup sugar
Pinch of salt
5 tablespoons cornstarch
2 cans (1 lb. each) grapefruit sections

Maraschino cherries, for garnish
¼ cup pecan halves, for garnish
Single crust pastry, extra thick
Pastry for trim on edge of pie
Love
Patience

Thy plants are an orchard of pomegranates, with pleasant fruits; camphire, with spikenard. Song of Sol. 4:13

Melt red hots in juice and add to the mixture of sugar, salt, and cornstarch. Bring it to a boil. Pour this over the grapefruit sections that have been placed in an unbaked pie shell. Garnish with pecan halves and cherries. Bake at 375 degrees until done, about 30 to 40 minutes. Remove from the oven and cool before serving.

189

TEXAS PECAN PIE

1½ cups pecan halves	1 cup light corn syrup
1 9-inch unbaked pastry shell	½ teaspoon vanilla
3 eggs, beaten	1 cup sugar
1 tablespoon margarine	1 tablespoon flour
Love	Patience

Arrange pecan halves in the bottom of the unbaked pastry shell. (Since pecan pie is a rather "heavy" pie, make a thicker pie shell than ordinarily used. If frozen pie shell is used, use both layers.) Combine eggs, margarine, corn syrup, and vanilla, stirring until well blended. Combine sugar and flour and add to egg mixture. Stir. Pour over pecans in pastry shell. Let stand until pecans rise to the surface. Bake in a moderate oven, 350 degrees, for 45 minutes.

190

CHOCOLATE AND WHITE COMBINATION CAKE

1 package white cake mix	1 package devil's food cake mix
Love	White icing, double recipe
Patience	

Following directions on each cake mix box, prepare batter for each cake. Place the devil's food cake in two square cake pans. Place the white cake mix in two round pans. Bake according to instructions. Use the chocolate cake as the base. Place white cake layers in the middle and on top of the square ones. Pleases everyone. Ice with double recipe of white prepared icing and decorate with just about anything the kids will like.

We have used glitters in different colors, cherries, pecans, and coconut. Place an American flag in the center.

DOUGHNUT CAKE

3 or 4 boxes cake-type
  doughnuts
Chocolate frosting mix
White frosting mix
Package moist coconut
Love

Cake decorations such as
  green and red crystals or
  pellets
Pecan pieces
1 bottle maraschino cherries
  ries
Patience

Ice some doughnuts with chocolate frosting, some with white frosting, or tinted pink or yellow from white frosting mix. Leave some doughnuts plain for those who prefer plain ones. Decorate some with coconut; others with cake decorations; others with pecan pieces. Stack pyramid fashion. Place cherries here and there for garnish. Each person may select the doughnut preferred when the cake is taken apart instead of sliced.

GINGERBREAD CUT-OUTS

⅓ cup water
1 package gingerbread
  mix
Love
Patience

For decoration:
  Whole cloves
  Raisins
  Icing
  Nuts
  Semisweets
  Small candies

*Not slothful in
business; fer-
vent in spirit;
serving the
Lord.
Rom. 12:11*

*Idle time is a
disguised
opportunity.*

Add ⅓ cup water to gingerbread mix. Keep blending until smooth. Chill in the refrigerator for 1 to 2 hours. Remove and roll dough out ⅛-inch thick. Use a gingerbread man cookie cutter which has been floured.

Lightly grease a cookie sheet and bake gingerbread men about 10 minutes at 375 degrees. This recipe will make 2½ to 3 dozen cookies.

PINEAPPLE UPSIDE-DOWN CAKE

1 cup (2 sticks) butter or
  margarine
1 box (1 lb.) brown sugar
1 large can (20 oz.) sliced
  pineapple

1 bottle (8 oz.) maraschino
  cherries
1 box yellow cake mix
Love
Patience

192

Into a shallow baking pan, pour melted butter or margarine. Spread brown sugar over butter. Place pineapple and cherries in decorative design in brown sugar and butter mixture. Prepare yellow cake mix according to instructions on the box and pour in pan over other ingredients. Preheat oven for 10 minutes at 375 degrees and bake cake for 30 minutes or until cake is brown. Turn out on waxed paper and cool.

POUND CAKE

1 cup butter
1⅔ cups sugar
4 drops almond flavoring
4 large eggs
¼ teaspoon salt
Love

2 cups (level) all-purpose
  flour, unsifted
2 teaspoons vanilla
Nutmeg or mace (optional)
Patience

Combine butter, sugar, and almond flavoring, mixing until very smooth. Add eggs, one at a time, mixing after each addition. Add salt. Flour need not be sifted and should be added gradually, ½ cup at a time. Add vanilla just before last addition of flour. (Add nutmeg or mace if desired.)

Lightly grease and flour angel food cake pan while oven is preheating to 350 degrees. Pour batter into pan and bake 30 minutes. Reduce heat to 300 degrees so cake won't over-brown before it is done. Cook 30 minutes more—total cooking time 1 hour.

LEMON-COCONUT ICING

(for Pound Cake)

1¾ cups sifted confectioners' sugar
¼ cup melted butter or
  margarine
¼ cup lemon juice
1 tablespoon cream
⅛ teaspoon grated lemon
  peel

1¾ cups sifted confectioners' sugar
1 package moist coconut
Maraschino cherries for
  garnish
Walnut halves for garnish

Combine 1¾ cups sugar with butter or margarine, lemon juice, cream, and lemon peel; beat until smooth. Add remaining 1¾ cups sugar; beat until smooth and of spreading consistency. Spread onto cake generously. Sprinkle iced cake all over with coconut. Garnish with cherries and walnuts.

SPICE CAKE

1 package spice cake mix	Cinnamon to taste
⅓ cup pecans	¼ cup confectioners' sugar
⅓ cup raisins	Pecans or walnuts for gar-
Love	nish
	Patience

Follow the directions on the spice cake mix package, adding 1 extra teaspoon of water. Mix in pecans and raisins. Bake according to directions. When done, allow to cool. Remove to cake platter and sprinkle with a little cinnamon and confectioners' sugar. Garnish with pecans or walnuts, if desired.

STRAWBERRY LONG CAKE

2 boxes yellow (or white) cake mix	1 pint whipping cream, whipped
2 packages (10 oz. each) of frozen sliced strawberries	Love
	Patience

194

Follow directions on the cake mix box for layer cake. Two boxes will make four layers.

Thaw strawberries; retain juice. After cake layers cool,

place strawberries with juice on one layer. Cover strawberries with whipped cream. Add another cake layer and repeat the above procedure. Decorate the topmost layer with additional strawberries.

SWISS STRAWBERRY CHEESE CAKE

3 packages (8-oz. each)
  cream cheese
1 cup sugar
3 eggs

½ cup (1 stick) butter, melted
1 teaspoon vanilla

LINING CRUST:

1 cup sugar
2 cups shortening

3 cups flour

TOPPING:

1 cup dairy sour cream
2 tablespoons sugar
½ teaspoon vanilla
Love

1 pkg. whole frozen strawberries
Patience

Mix cream cheese and sugar in mixer at medium speed until mixture begins to cream; then add eggs, melted butter, and vanilla. Continue to mix at medium speed until mixture is very creamy. Pour into a cake pan that is lined on the bottom and sides with any good sugar cookie dough. Preheat oven to 450 degrees. Put cake in oven and bake for 15 minutes or more until cake rises ½ inch above the pan. The top of the cake can be decorated with the strawberry-sour cream topping mixture after it is removed from oven. The old 1–2–3 sugar cookie dough can be used for the lining: 1 lb. sugar, 2 lbs. shortening, and 3 lbs. flour.

195

APRICOT MERINGUE TORTE

CAKE:

¼ cup margarine
½ cup sugar
2 egg yolks
1¾ cups sifted cake flour
2 teaspoons baking pow-
    der
Dash of salt

½ cup milk
¼ teaspoon vanilla
¼ teaspoon almond
    extract
2 egg whites
½ cup sugar
Love
Patience

FILLING:

½ pound dried apricots
2 cups water
1 cup sugar
1 cup heavy cream,
    whipped

¼ cup broken walnut
    pieces
Apricot halves for garnish,
    optional

Cream together margarine and ½ cup sugar. Add egg
yolks, one at a time, beating well after each addition. Add
sifted dry ingredients alternately with milk, vanilla, and
almond extract. Spread in two waxed-paper-lined 8-inch
round pans.

Whip egg whites and remaining ½ cup sugar to make
meringue; spread over one layer of cake batter. Bake
both layers in moderate oven of 350 degrees for about 40
minutes. Allow to cool.

Prepare the filling by cooking dried apricots in 2 cups
of water. Simmer until apricots are tender which will take
about 25–30 minutes. Add 1 cup sugar and boil for about
5 minutes. Mash the apricots coarsely, and allow to
cool. Then fold in 1 cup heavy cream, which has been
whipped (retain a little whipped cream for top of cake).

Place filling between layers of cake, having meringue
layer on top. Sprinkle walnut pieces over top and spoon

on the whipped cream. Garnish with halves of apricots.

If desired, this recipe may be doubled. Use 4 cake pans, of course, which will give you another layer of meringue in the middle of the cake.

BANANAS MEDITERRANEAN

6 bananas, large and yel-
low
Lemon juice
1 cup brown sugar
½ cup butter
Love

¼ cup coconut
Cinnamon
Cinnamon sticks for gar-
nish
Vanilla ice cream
(optional)
Patience

Peel bananas and halve them lengthwise. Brush well with lemon juice. Melt brown sugar and butter in a saucepan or chafing dish. Add bananas. Cook about 5 minutes. Sprinkle with coconut and cinnamon. Serve immediately. Bananas Mediterranean is also excellent as a topping on vanilla ice cream—a Banana Mediterranean Sundae. Serves 6.

CHERRY MERINGUES

MERINGUES:

6 egg whites
1½ teaspoons lemon juice
2 cups sugar
Love
Patience

CHERRY FILLING:

2 cans (1 lb. each) cherries,
sweetened and pitted
¼ cup sugar
¼ teaspoon cinnamon
½ cup powdered sugar

Judge not, that ye be not judged. Matt. 7:1

When we spend our time criti-cizing others, they will spend their time criti-cizing us . . . filling the cosmic aura surrounding our lives with negative forces. Remember, if someone has bad things to say about you, live in such a way that no one will believe him.

197

Heat oven to 275 to 300 degrees. Beat egg whites until fluffy. Add lemon juice and beat again. Beat in sugar, a small amount at a time, until very stiff. Cover a baking sheet with brown paper, drop meringue by the spoonsful in high heaps. With edge of spoon make a hollow center in each heap. Place meringues in the oven and bake for 40 minutes; reduce heat to 250 degrees and bake 10 minutes longer. Meringues should be very light brown and firm.

For filling, mix cherries and sugar and cinnamon together. Pile into the centers of meringues (and around them if served on a large plate). Sprinkle cherry-filled meringues with powdered sugar.

FRUIT-COCONUT DESSERT IN MELON HALVES

2 or 3 (depending on number of diners—2 will make 4 melon bowls, 3 will serve 6) honeydew melons, cut in half and chilled
Seedless green grapes, chilled
Canned fruit cocktail, chilled
Canned peach halves
Maraschino cherries
1 can of mandarin orange sections
1 package of moist coconut
Vanilla ice cream
Whipping cream (optional)
Love
Patience

Cut melons in half. Remove seeds and center pulp. With a melon ball scoop remove balls of melon and mix with grapes, fruit cocktail, peach halves, maraschino cherries, and mandarin orange sections. Drain thoroughly. Mix in part of the coconut. Place one peach half in the bottom inside of each melon. Place one or two scoops of ice cream into the peach half; fill each melon half with mixed fruit. Top with half of peach, cherries, and more coconut. Whipping cream may be added, if desired. This is a very versatile dessert. Any kind of melon may be hollowed out to serve as a bowl for dessert. For a party a watermelon may be used, or pineapples or cantaloupes for individual servings. Any combination of fruits, canned or fresh, may be combined with the melon and ice cream to produce attractive and delicious desserts.

BROILED GRAPEFRUIT NORTHERN

3 or 4 grapefruit, cut into halves
Brown sugar, 6 to 8 tablespoons
Several pats of butter

Honey, 6 to 8 tablespoons
Blueberries, 6 to 8 teaspoons
Love
Patience

Butter and honey shall he eat, that he may know to refuse the evil, and choose the good.
Isa. 7:15

Trim edges of halves of grapefruit to make a scalloped border. Sprinkle each half with brown sugar. Place a pat of butter on each one and pour about a tablespoon of honey over each grapefruit half. Place in oven with slow temperature and broil for about 15 minutes, until brown sugar has glazed and butter has melted. Remove. Garnish each grapefruit center with a teaspoon of blueberries.

CRÊPES D'ORANGE

1 cup sifted flour
6 tablespoons confectioners' sugar
½ teaspoon salt

1 cup milk
2 eggs
Love
Patience

199

Sift flour, confectioners' sugar, and salt together. Add milk and stir until completely smooth. Add eggs and beat thoroughly. Pour batter from pitcher or large spoon onto lightly greased hot griddle. When pancakes are puffed and full of bubbles, after 1 or 2 minutes, turn and cook about 1 minute on second side. Spread crêpes with Orange Hard Sauce; roll. Serve crêpes warm. Garnish with cherries.

ORANGE HARD SAUCE

½ cup butter
1 package (1 lb.) superfine
  sugar
Grated rind of 3 oranges
Love

½ teaspoon salt
Juice of three oranges
Cherries, for garnish,
  (optional)
Patience

Combine butter, sugar, orange rind, and salt. *Beat well.* Add orange juice gradually and blend thoroughly.

ORANGE-NUT FROZEN SUNDAE

18 marshmallows, cut in
  small pieces
1 cup orange juice, made
  double strength from frozen juice concentrate
1 cup small pieces of peanut brittle

1 cup cream, whipped
Orange slices or sections,
  extra crushed peanut
  brittle, and cherries for
  garnish
Love
Patience

200

Soak marshmallows in orange juice for about 30 minutes. Fold this and peanut brittle pieces into whipped cream. Place in refrigerator tray; freeze for several hours. Serve as you would ice cream; garnish with slices or sections of oranges, a few pieces of crushed peanut brittle, and cherries.

FRESH PEACH BROIL

6 ripe large peaches (Free-
  stone, preferably)
1 tablespoon lemon juice
¼ cup light brown sugar
Love

Maraschino cherries (op-
  tional)
2 tablespoons butter
Dash cinnamon
Patience

Habit is the enemy of thought.

Peel and slice 6 large peaches into halves. Remove pits. Put peaches into a buttered casserole dish or pie plate. Sprinkle each peach half with ¼ teaspoon lemon juice and 1 teaspoon light brown sugar. (If cherries are desired place them into center of peach half.) Dot with butter and a dash of cinnamon. Oven should be 325 degrees. Bake for 10 minutes until soft. Then put the peaches under the broiler for a few minutes until brown.

PEACH WAFFLE SHORTCAKE, BOSTON

1 package frozen waffles
¼ cup confectioners'
  sugar
1 can (16 oz.) sliced
  peaches, drained
Love

1 pint whipping cream,
  whipped
Maraschino cherries for
  garnish
Spiced peaches for topping
  and garnish
Patience

201

On a flat serving plate or platter arrange waffle squares, toasted and sprinkled with confectioners' sugar. On waffles place a layer of sliced peaches and then a layer of whipped cream. Repeat the process until waffles are used, and top the whole dessert with whipped cream. Garnish with cherries and spiced peaches. Serve with extra ingredients: cherries, spiced peaches, whipping cream.

PEACH MELBA

1 qt. vanilla ice cream	Melba Sauce
6 peach halves	6 tablespoons walnuts, broken pieces
Love	Patience

Top each generous dip of vanilla ice cream with a peach half. Pour Melba Sauce over and around the peach halves. Sprinkle with walnut pieces. Serves 6.

If you find it difficult to meditate for lack of solitude, just wash the dishes.

MELBA SAUCE:

1 cup thawed frozen raspberries with juice	1 teaspoon sugar
	1 teaspoon cornstarch
Love	½ cup red currant jelly
	Patience

Combine raspberries with juice, sugar, and cornstarch in a saucepan and cook slowly over lowest heat until clear. Strain through fine sieve. Cool. Blend in red currant jelly. Makes 1 cup.

202

CHARLOTTE RUSSE ECONOMY

1 box (10 oz.) frozen strawberries, drained	1½ pints commercial sour cream
Love	1 cup brown sugar
	Patience

Place drained frozen strawberries into a baking dish. Cover strawberries thoroughly with the sour cream. Top the sour cream with brown sugar. Place into a preheated oven at 350 degrees and bake until bubbling, about 20–25 minutes. Serve in dessert glasses. Can be served hot or cold. Makes 4–6 servings.

ICE CREAM SUNDAE PIE

2–3 packages ladyfingers
1 quart chocolate ice cream
1 quart strawberry ice cream
1 quart lime sherbet
Love

Apricot preserves (or pineapple)
Cherry preserves (or strawberry)
Pecan pieces
Maraschino cherries (optional)
Patience

Just before serving, arrange ladyfingers on a chilled metal server (metal keeps ice cream cold longer) in the shape of pie crust. Make a pyramid of ice cream by the following instructions: With an ice cream dipper, dip chocolate ice cream and arrange in first pyramid layer; then dip strawberry ice cream into another section of pyramid dips; and lime sherbet in the same pattern. Spoon apricot preserves (or pineapple if preferred) onto the strawberry and chocolate ice cream; cherry preserves (or strawberry if preferred) onto the lime sherbet and strawberry ice cream. Sprinkle pecans over top. Add cherries if desired.

The thing that hath been, it is that which shall be; and that which is done is that which shall be done: and there is no new thing under the sun. Eccles. 1:9

Everything good and worthwhile starts with a thought that is then amplified with energy and communication.

203

POTS DE CRÈME

1 cup (1 6-oz. package)
semisweet chocolate
pieces
1¼ cups light cream
2 egg yolks
(Save the whites if you
wish to top this dessert
with meringue)
Love

Dash of salt
¼ teaspoon vanilla
Whipping cream
(optional for topping)
Maraschino cherries (op-
tional)
Slivered almonds (option-
al)
Patience

Combine the chocolate pieces and cream in a saucepan.
Stir over low heat. Melt and blend until smooth and
slick-looking. Do not let mixture boil, but allow to
thicken slightly. Beat egg yolks and salt until yolks reach
a thick lemony texture. Stir chocolate mixture into the
beaten egg yolks. Add vanilla and stir until blended.

Spoon Pots de Crème into sherbet dishes or small
bowls, and chill, covered, until of thick pudding consistency. (Before chilling you may top with meringue or
whipped cream, if desired.)

When ready to serve, garnish with maraschino cherries
and slivered almonds, if desired.

ITALIAN CUSTARD

1½ cups sugar
4 eggs
¼ cup sugar
3 cups milk
Love

1 teaspoon vanilla
Dash of rum flavoring (op-
tional)
Whole walnuts or pecans
Patience

204

Melt 1½ cups sugar in a skillet until sugar begins to become dark. Stir. Keep the sugar moving around in the

skillet and remove it shortly before it is thoroughly darkened. (It will cook a while after removal from the heat.) Pour into 8 oven custard dishes. Roll the liquid sugar around in each dish to get syrup distributed on the sides of the dishes. Mix together the eggs, sugar, milk, vanilla, and rum flavoring, if desired. Pour into the oven dishes over the syrup. Drop 3 or 4 walnuts on top of each custard. (These will be on bottom when eaten.) Place custard dishes in a pan of hot water and bake in a preheated 325-degree oven for about 1 hour. (Custard is done when a silver knife inserted into it comes out clean.) Just before serving, unmold. Syrup on the bottom will roll down the sides and surround the cooked custard. Best served cold.

FRENCH QUARTER PRALINES

3 cups sugar
¾ cup canned evaporated
  milk
Love

¼ cup water
2 cups pecans, large pieces
Patience

Caramelize 1 cup of sugar by heating slowly in a heavy skillet. Stir only after sugar begins to melt, then occasionally. While sugar is melting, pour milk and water into a heavy pan. Begin to heat milk; do not allow to boil. Meanwhile, the caramelizing sugar will be melting into a smooth, slick, heavy liquid mixture. When this sugar is entirely melted, with no lumps and no bubbles, pour it into the kettle with milk. (Do not pour sugar unless it is free of lumps and bubbles.) Sugar may form a large hard lump when it mixes with milk—this will dissolve. When

The most valuable commodity in the world is time. How we utilize time reflects our philosophy. When you occupy someone else's time in idle gossip, you are stealing the greatest jewel in his treasure house.

205

the sugar is well on its way to dissolving in the milk, add the rest of the sugar, a half cup at a time, stirring after each addition.

Pralines should cook at a medium heat. When candy has reached a rolling, foamy consistency, test in a glass of cold water. If test forms a *decidedly hard* ball, remove from heat and place the kettle in a large pan or sink of cool water. Add the pecans and stir thoroughly. It is not necessary to beat. Stir occasionally until candy thickens and crackles when stirred. Then it is ready to dip by the teaspoonfuls onto waxed paper. Mixture can be replaced on very low heat if it hardens before all of the recipe is dipped, and the remainder dipped from the warm kettle.

MIAMI BEACH LIME CHIFFON DESSERT

1 tablespoon (1 envelope) unflavored gelatin
½ cup sugar
¼ teaspoon salt
4 egg yolks
½ cup lime juice
¼ cup water
1½ teaspoons grated lime peel
Love

2 or 3 drops green food coloring
4 egg whites
½ cup sugar
1 cup heavy cream, whipped
1 or 2 drops green food coloring
Lime wedges or slices
Patience

Thoroughly mix gelatin, ½ cup sugar, and salt in saucepan. Beat together egg yolks, lime juice, and water; stir into gelatin mixture. Cook over medium heat, stirring until mixture comes to a boil. Remove from heat; stir in grated lime peel. Add 2 or 3 drops green food coloring to tint light shade of green. Chill; stir occasionally. When lime mixture thickens enough to form a mound when dropped from a spoon, beat egg whites till soft peaks form; gradually add ½ cup sugar, beating to stiff peaks. Fold gelatin mixture into egg whites. Fold in part of whipped cream, reserving about ¼ for topping. Spoon into dessert dishes or large serving dish. Chill until firm. Spread with more whipped cream to which 1 or 2 drops of green food coloring have been added. Trim with lime wedges, or slices.

HOT APPLESAUCE COMPOTE

1 can (16 oz.) applesauce	½ apple, cut into 4
4 tablespoons red hots	wedges, with core
(Cinnamon Imperials)	trimmed out
Love	**Patience**

Heat applesauce and place into compote dishes. Sprinkle a tablespoon of red hots into each serving of applesauce and top with a wedge of apple.

FRUIT COCKTAIL ORANGE JELLO

3 packages (3 oz. each)	3 or 4 oranges
orange jello	1 small package marshmal-
1 can (16 oz.) fruit cocktail	lows
Love	**Patience**

207

Prepare orange jello as directed on the package, mixing in the fruit cocktail as suggested in the package directions.

Allow to chill in cups which are easy for children to handle. Retain the extra fruit cocktail.

When ready to serve, place marshmallows on top. Cut oranges into small wedges (so they may be eaten too, if desired). Place the extra fruit cocktail inside orange wedges. Garnish with marshmallows.

Beverages

Let your light so shine before men, that they may see your good works, and glorify your Father which is in heaven.
Matt. 5:16

Each day, build a spiritual temple for the Lord. Let the warm glow of your love shine through the windows upon each soul you meet. Kneel at the altar in constant prayer. Your faith in Him is the foundation. Open the door to the needy with charity. Your thoughts can be the steeple, always directed toward heaven. Fill the sanctuary with music from your heart. Provide a room for the study of His word.

If you really want to discover the presence of the Lord, take on a project too large for you to handle and pray about it.

SUNRISE SUNDAY MORNING

3 cups chilled tomato juice
1½ tablespoons lemon or lime juice
2 teaspoons sugar

¼ teaspoon salt
¼ teaspoon M.S.G. powder
9 drops Tabasco sauce
Lemon slices

Combine all ingredients together. Pour into chilled glasses and garnish with lemon slices. Serves 4.

For I was an hungred, and ye gave me meat: I was thirsty, and ye gave me drink: I was a stranger, and ye took me in. Matt. 25:35

SUNSET BOUILLON

1 quart cut-up fresh tomatoes (about 6 large)
1 cup chicken stock

1 teaspoon salt
⅛ teaspoon black pepper
Dash of red pepper

Cook tomatoes in chicken stock until soft. Press through sieve. Heat liquid and seasonings. Serve hot. Serves 6.

THE VEGETARIAN

2 cups tomato juice
½ teaspoon salt
2 tablespoons lemon juice
1 teaspoon Worcestershire powder
3 sprigs parsley

1 small stalk celery, cut into 2-inch pieces
1 small raw carrot, cut into 2-inch pieces
1 slice onion
4 ice cubes

211

Put all ingredients except ice cubes in blender container; cover and run on speed 7 (or high) until vegetables are liquefied. While blender is running, add ice cubes, one at a time. Serves 6.

APPLE VALLEY STEAMER

4 cups apple juice
1 cup water
½ cup firmly packed brown sugar
½ cup orange juice

3 tablespoons lemon juice
¼ teaspoon nutmeg
1 3-inch stick cinnamon
Thin orange or lemon slices (optional)

Combine apple juice, water, brown sugar, orange juice, lemon juice, nutmeg, and cinnamon in a 2-quart saucepan. Set over medium heat and stir until sugar is dissolved. Bring to boiling; reduce heat and simmer 15 minutes. Strain through a fine sieve into heated serving cups. If desired, garnish with thin orange or lemon slices. Serves 8.

CHRISTMAS CHEER

4 cups apple cider
2 cups bottled cranberry juice
1 cup orange juice
1 can (12 oz.) apricot nectar

1 lemon
36 whole cloves
10 sugar lumps (optional)
1 teaspoon cinnamon (optional)

212

In a large saucepan, combine cider, cranberry juice, orange juice, and apricot nectar. Wash lemon; cut thinly into 12 slices. Insert 3 cloves in each slice; add to fruit juices. Over very low heat, bring just to simmer—15 to 20 minutes. Pour into punch bowl. In small bowl, toss sugar lumps with cinnamon. Drop a sugar lump into each punch cup. Makes 10 6-ounce servings.

MISSIONARY PUNCH

1 quart boiling water
2 teaspoons instant tea
2 cups water
¾ cup sugar
1 teaspoon whole cloves
1 3-inch stick cinnamon

2 6-oz. or 1 12-oz. can
  frozen orange juice
  concentrate
1 6-oz. can frozen grape-
  fruit juice concentrate
Cloves
Orange Slices

Add boiling water to tea in large bowl; set aside. Simmer 2 cups water with sugar, 1 teaspoon whole cloves, and cinnamon stick for 10 minutes. Strain into tea. Reconstitute frozen juices; add to tea. Reheat. Serve in bowl with clove-studded orange slices. Makes 30 punch-cup servings.

Vanity of vanities, saith the Preacher, vanity of vanities; all is vanity.
Eccles. 1:2

A true sign that one lacks humility is when he or she gazes into a mirror and says, "There is indeed an humble person."

SKIER'S ROMANCE

6 egg yolks
¾ cup sugar
⅛ teaspoon salt
1 tablespoon angostura
  bitters

6 stiffly beaten egg whites
4 cups scalded milk
Grated nutmeg

In medium-sized glass or ceramic punch bowl, beat egg yolks with ½ cup sugar, salt, and bitters until fluffy. Add remaining sugar to stiffly beaten egg whites, beating in until smooth. Fold into first mixture. Beat scalded milk with rotary beater and stir gradually into the egg mixture. Ladle at once from bowl into mugs. Sprinkle top of each mug with a few grains of nutmeg. Makes 8 to 10 servings.

213

STEAMY APRICOT MIST

1 cup water
2 tablespoons sugar
4 whole cloves

1 3-inch stick cinnamon
1½ cups (1 12-oz. can)
  apricot nectar
2 tablespoons lemon juice

Combine water, sugar, cloves, and cinnamon in a small saucepan. Set over low heat and stir until sugar is dissolved. Increase heat and bring to boiling. Boil gently for 5 minutes. Add the apricot nectar and lemon juice. Continue to heat until very hot. Remove spices and serve immediately. Serves 4.
NOTE: Beverage may be chilled and served over ice cubes.

WINTER FRIENDSHIP CUP

6 cups boiling water
6 tea bags
2 teaspoons grated lemon
  peel
2 teaspoons grated orange
  peel
½ cup fresh orange juice

¼ cup lemon juice
½ cup pineapple juice
Sugar to taste
8 to 10 thin slices lemon
  stuck with 3 or 4 cloves
  each
8 to 10 long cinnamon
  sticks

214

Pour boiling water over tea bags in large teapot. Brew 5 minutes. Remove tea bags. In enamel, agate, or glass saucepan combine peels and fruit juices, adding sugar to taste. Simmer gently 5 minutes. Pour mixture into teapot. Serve hot in mugs with a clove-studded lemon slice and a cinnamon stick in each one. Makes 8 to 10 mugs.

GERMAN MOCHA

1½ teaspoons instant coffee dissolved in 1 cup warm water, or extra-strength brewed coffee

Rich milk
Whipping cream, whipped

Add rich milk to extra-strong coffee. Stir and add whipping cream drifts to float on top. Serve from cups or mugs. Serves 1.

HOT MOCHA DRINK

6 cups milk
½ cup instant cocoa mix
¼ cup instant coffee

Cinnamon-sugar to taste
Marshmallows

Heat milk in a saucepan. Do not boil, but cook to point of scalding. Add instant cocoa mix and stir. Add instant coffee and stir. When completely blended, remove from heat and beat until frothy. Pour into serving glasses or cups and sprinkle with cinnamon-sugar. Top with marshmallows. Serve hot. Serves 6.

I am come into my garden, my sister, my spouse: I have gathered my myrrh with my spice; I have eaten my honeycomb with my honey; I have drunk my wine with my milk: eat, O friends; drink, yea, drink abundantly, O beloved.
Song of Sol. 5:1

LOUISIANA COFFEE CREOLE

Extra strong pot of coffee
1 cup whipping cream
Cinnamon to taste
Nutmeg to taste

4 tablespoons confectioners' sugar
Maraschino cherries, optional

Pour strong coffee into cups—about ¾ full. Whip cream with cinnamon, nutmeg, and confectioners' sugar. Top coffee with ¼ cup of spiced whipped cream. Place a cherry on top of each cup and serve.

THE BEACHCOMBER

¼ cup frozen orange-
grapefruit-juice
concentrate
¾ cup ice water

1 pint lemon sherbet
1 bottle (12 oz.) ginger ale,
chilled

Pour frozen orange-grapefruit-juice concentrate into an electric mixer. Add ice water and sherbet. Cover and blend about 15 seconds. Divide mixture among 4 chilled glasses. Slowly pour in ginger ale to fill each glass. Stir gently and serve right away. Serves 4.

BRAZILIAN CREAM DELIGHT

1½ cups cold coffee
beverage
1 cup apricot nectar,
chilled

⅔ cup cold milk
1 pint (2 cups) coffee ice
cream, softened

Mix coffee, apricot nectar, and milk in a large bowl. Add softened ice cream to milk mixture and beat with a rotary beater until smooth. Serve immediately in tall glasses. Serves 4.

BRUNCH PUNCH

2 cups strong hot tea
1 cup sugar
1 cup orange juice

½ cup lemon juice
1 pint chilled ginger ale
1 pint orange sherbet

216

Pour hot tea over sugar; stir until sugar dissolves; add juices. Refrigerate until chilled. Then pour into punch bowl. Add ginger ale. Spoon on sherbet. Makes 16 servings.

CARNIVAL IN JULY

1½ cups whipping cream
1 egg
¾ cup canned or cooked fresh blueberries with syrup

2 tablespoons sugar
2 cups milk
½ pint vanilla ice cream

In a chilled bowl whip cream with electric mixer until it will hold soft peaks; set aside. Put egg, blueberries with syrup, sugar, and milk in blender container; cover and run on speed 7 (or high) until very smooth. Pour carefully over whipped cream and gently fold together. Pour into 6 glasses; top each with a scoop of ice cream. Serves 6.

FROSTED COFFEE

2 cups strong coffee,* chilled
¾ cup chocolate milk

1½ cups soft coffee ice cream

Life is like a great symphony: All of the parts must be played in harmony.

Combine coffee, milk, and 1 cup ice cream in medium bowl; beat with rotary beater just until smooth. Pour into 3 or 4 tall glasses. Top with rest of ice cream. Serves 4.
* Use 2 tablespoons instant coffee, dissolved in 2 cups boiling water.

RASPBERRY RHAPSODY

1 cup pineapple juice, chilled
½ cup frozen raspberries, thawed

1 pint lemon sherbet, cut into chunks

217

Put pineapple juice and raspberries in blender container; cover and run on speed 7 (or high) until raspberries are liquefied. Strain to remove seeds. Return mixture to blender container; add sherbet; cover and run on speed 5 (or high) until smooth. Makes 4 servings.

SUNDAY CIRCUS

3 cups orange juice
1 cup canned fruit
  cocktail, drained

1 pint vanilla ice cream

Put orange juice and fruit cocktail in blender container; cover and run on speed 4 (or low) until fruit is finely chopped. Pour into 4 tall glasses; top each with a scoop of ice cream. Serves 4.

SUNDAY TODDY

1 chilled jar drained
  prunes (baby pack)
⅓ cup chilled orange
  juice
1 cup cold milk
Pinch salt

1 teaspoon lemon juice
1 tablespoon sugar
1 big scoop vanilla ice
  cream
Orange peel

218

Mix prunes, orange juice, and milk. Add salt, lemon juice, sugar, and ice cream. Beat to blend; pour into glasses. Top each with twist of orange peel. Makes 4 small servings.

SWEET PEACH

1 package (10 oz.) frozen
    sliced peaches, thawed
¼ cup lemon juice

2 tablespoons honey
1 pint vanilla ice cream,
    cut into chunks

Put all ingredients in blender container; cover and run on speed 7 (or high) until smooth and thick. If necessary, stop blender during processing and push ingredients toward blades with rubber spatula. Pour into tall glasses. Serves 4.

THE TEEN QUEEN

2 packages (10 oz. each)
    frozen red raspberries,
    thawed and sieved

1 quart vanilla ice cream
3 cups cold milk

Add raspberries to half the ice cream; beat until smooth. Add milk and blend. Pour into 6 chilled 10-ounce glasses. Top each with scoop of remaining ice cream. Serves 6.

The noblest of all possessions is character. The noblest trait of character is faithfulness. There can be no greatness without character. There can be no character without love. Character is not inherited nor is it a gift. It is victory over one's self.

VELVET MALT SUPREME

4 egg yolks
4 cups cold milk
½ cup chocolate malted
    milk powder

¼ teaspoon nutmeg
¼ cup chilled whipping
    cream
Semi-sweet chocolate

219

Beat egg yolks until thick and lemon-colored. Add milk, malted milk powder, and nutmeg. Beat until well blended. Using a chilled bowl and beater, whip cream. Pour the beverage into chilled glasses and top each serving with about 2 tablespoons of the whipped cream. Garnish with chocolate curls made by pulling chocolate block across a shredder. Serves 4.

VOLCANO

6 cups (1 46-oz. can) red
  Hawaiian fruit punch,
  chilled
¾ cup lemon juice

1 quart vanilla ice cream
2 bottles (7 oz. each)
  lemon-lime carbonated
  beverage, chilled
Lemon peel

Combine punch and lemon juice. Spoon about half the ice cream into chilled tall glasses. Add half the punch; muddle with ice cream. Add remaining punch; tip each glass and pour carbonated beverage down side to fill. Top each with a scoop of ice cream. Trim with lemon peel. Serves 10.

BUTTERFLY SHAKE

220

1 cup cold milk
2 tablespoons orange juice

2 tablespoons honey
1 ripe banana, peeled and
  quartered

Put all ingredients in blender container; cover and run on speed 7 (or high) until smooth. Makes 2 servings.

GINGER FIZZ

1 egg white
2 tablespoons lemon juice
1 tablespoon sugar

½ cup crushed ice
Ginger ale, chilled
Maraschino cherry

Put all ingredients except ginger ale in blender container; cover and run on speed 6 (or high) until frothy. Pour into a glass; add ginger ale. Garnish with a maraschino cherry. Makes 1 serving.

GRAPE HAWAIIAN PUNCH

1½ cups frozen orange
  juice concentrate
1 cup bottled lemon juice
2½ cups chilled grape
  juice

½ cup sugar, or to taste
3½ cups ice water
1 cup crushed pineapple
Cracked ice

Mix all of the above ingredients. Pour into pitcher over cracked ice. Serves 6.

HAPPY HOLIDAYS

1⅓ cups tea, chilled
3 tablespoons sugar
¼ cup lemon juice
⅔ cup orange juice,
  chilled

1 can (12 oz.) apricot nectar, chilled
1 bottle (7 oz.) ginger ale, chilled
Ice cubes
6 fresh mint sprigs

And again I say unto you, It is easier for a camel to go through the eye of a needle, than for a rich man to enter into the kingdom of God. Matt. 19:24

221

Combine tea, sugar, juices, and nectar; stir to mix well. Gradually add ginger ale. Serve over ice in tall glasses, each garnished with mint sprig. Makes 6 servings.

ICED TEA, WITH SPICE

8 glasses regular recipe for
   tea
¼ cup frozen lemonade
   concentrate
¼ cup frozen orange juice
   concentrate

Cinnamon to taste
Dash of cloves
Brown sugar to taste
Lemon slices

Mix the tea, lemonade and orange juice concentrates. Add spices and sugar. Taste. Adjust spices and sugar to taste. Serve with lemon slices. Makes 8 large servings.

ISLAND MINT JULEP

6 sprigs fresh mint
¾ cup sugar
¾ cup lemon juice

3 cups unsweetened pine-
   apple juice
3 cups ginger ale
Sprigs of mint for garnish

Wash mint leaves; bruise with spoon; cover with sugar. Add lemon juice; let stand about 15 minutes; add pine-apple juice. Pour over ice in pitcher or tall glasses; add ginger ale. Garnish with sprigs of mint. Serve straws with these. Makes about 8 servings.

KENTUCKY PUNCH

1 cup lime juice
1 cup orange juice
1 cup granulated sugar
1 jar (8 oz.) maraschino
   cherries

8 dashes angostura bitters
1 tray ice cubes
Orange and lime slices

222

In blender or drink shaker, combine lime juice, orange juice, sugar, 1½ teaspoons maraschino-cherry juice, and bitters. Blend at low speed or shake for 1 minute. Pour over ice cubes in pitcher; stir well. Let stand 10 minutes. Strain into chilled glasses or small ceramic coconut shells. Garnish each with cherry, orange, and lime slice speared on fancy pick. Makes 4 6-ounce servings.

THE LEPRECHAUN

1 cup mint leaves	1 cup lime juice
1 cup sugar	¼ cup lemon juice
1 cup boiling water	Few drops green food
1 quart cold water	coloring
1¼ cups crushed ice	Sprigs of mint

Put mint leaves, sugar, and boiling water in blender container; cover and run on speed 5 (or high) until mint is chopped. Cool; strain into a large pitcher. Add cold water, crushed ice, fruit juices, and food coloring; mix well. Pour into ice cube-filled glasses and garnish with fresh mint. Makes 8 servings.

Prejudice is a fence of fear that we build around our small, small world.

THE MENEHUNE

½ cup sugar	2 unbeaten egg whites
⅔ cup water	4 cups finely crushed ice
⅔ cup unsweetened pine-apple juice	Mint sprigs for garnish
⅔ cup fresh lemon juice	Pineapple chunks for gar-nish
2 tablespoons fresh lime juice	

223

Combine sugar with water and heat for 10 minutes. Remove from heat and chill. Mix pineapple, lemon and lime juice together and add to syrup. Pour into shaker or blender. Last, add egg whites and ice. Shake or blend until smooth and creamy. Pour into frosted glasses and serve immediately. Garnish with mint sprigs threaded through pineapple chunks.

NAPA VALLEY COOLER

½ cup sugar
2 cups water
1 cup grape juice

1 cup orange juice
½ cup lemon juice
Ginger ale, if desired

Make a syrup of the sugar and water; cool. Add fruit juices. Mix well. Pour over ice in pitcher or tall glasses, adding some ginger ale if desired. Serve straws with these. Makes 6 to 8 servings.

THE SMILING CHERRY

1 cup water
½ cup sugar
1 cup double-strength tea, cooled
1 cup canned pitted sour cherries

¾ cup cherry juice
¼ cup lemon juice
2 tablespoons pineapple juice
1 quart cold water

Put 1 cup water and sugar in small saucepan; bring to a boil, stirring to dissolve sugar. Boil 5 minutes. Set aside to cool. Put tea, cherry juice, cherries, lemon juice, and pineapple juice in blender container; cover and run on speed 7 (or high) until cherries are liquefied. Pour into a pitcher; stir in syrup and 1 quart cold water. Chill. To serve, stir and pour over ice cubes in tall glasses. Makes 8 servings.

SONG OF CRANBERRY MOUNTAIN

2¼ cups cold water
½ cup lemon juice
2 cans (7 oz. each) jellied
   cranberry sauce

1 teaspoon almond extract
1 cup orange juice
1 bottle (6 oz.) ginger ale

Put cold water, lemon juice, cranberry sauce, and almond extract in blender container; cover and run on speed 7 (or high) until smooth. Pour into a pitcher or small punch bowl; stir in orange juice and ginger ale. To serve, pour over ice cubes in tall glasses. Makes 6 large servings.

SOUTHERN SMOOTHEE

1 cup milk
1 cup canned apricot
   halves or ½ cup soaked
   dried apricots

⅛ teaspoon almond
   extract
Sugar to taste
1 cup crushed ice

Put all ingredients in blender container; cover and run on speed 7 (or high) until smooth and ice is completely liquefied, about 30 seconds. Makes 2 cups.

SPARKLING PINK SURPRISE

1 package (16 oz.) frozen
   strawberries
1 quart cold water

2 cans (6 oz. each) frozen
   orange juice concentrate
1 quart carbonated water
10 to 12 sprigs of mint

Thaw strawberries according to directions on package. Force thawed strawberries through a sieve or food mill and set them aside. Pour water into a large bowl. Stir in orange juice concentrate. Add the sieved strawberries and their syrup. Just before serving, add and blend the carbonated water. Serve immediately over crushed ice in tall glasses. Garnish with sprigs of mint. Serves 12.

TEXAS COOLER

Mint and cherries
1½ cups orange juice
1 cup grapefruit juice
2 tablespoons lemon juice

2 tablespoons light corn syrup
1 pint ginger ale

Make ice cubes with pieces of mint and cherries in them. Blend orange, grapefruit, and lemon juice. Add corn syrup and mix thoroughly. Add ginger ale to fruit juices and pour mixture into glasses filled with ice cubes. Serve immediately.

THE TRADER

2 cups diced ripe canta-
loupe
¼ cup sugar
2 tablespoons lime juice

1 tablespoon lemon juice
Few grains salt
1 can (12 oz.) pineapple-
grapefruit drink, chilled

Combine cantaloupe, sugar, lime juice, lemon juice, and salt in a blender. After blending thoroughly, chill. Then stir in the chilled fruit drink and pour over crushed ice in frosted glasses. Serves 3.

APPLE JUICE

1 can (46 oz.) apple juice   Maraschino cherries
Apple slices

Apple juice can be served hot or cold. Delicious either way. Pour into a punch bowl and garnish with round apple slices which have been cored. Place a cherry atop each apple slice.

AUTUMN NOCTURNE

2 cans (12-oz. each) apricot nectar	1½ quarts sweet cider
1½ cups orange juice	20 maraschino cherries
¾ cup lemon juice	(optional)

Combine nectar, orange and lemon juices, and cider. Refrigerate until well chilled—at least 2 hours. Serve in punch cups. Garnish each with maraschino cherry, if desired. Makes 20 servings.

BOSTON HARBOR PUNCH

2 quarts water	4 cups strained orange juice
5 level tablespoons tea or 15 tea bags	1½ quarts grape juice
2 cups strained fresh lemon juice	2 cups sugar
	1 quart ginger ale

Bring 2 quarts freshly drawn cold water to full rolling boil in large saucepan. Remove from heat. Add tea immediately. Brew 4 minutes. Stir and then strain tea into glass pitcher holding all the remaining ingredients except ginger ale. Mix. Just before serving, pour mixture into punch bowl over block of ice. Stir in ginger ale. Makes about 50 punch cups.

Good builders create beautiful houses . . . good parents create beautiful homes.

CALIFORNIA CIDER

4 sticks cinnamon
24 whole cloves or 1 tea-
    spoon allspice
5 cups sweet cider or apple
    juice
4 cups grape juice
½ cup lemon juice

1 teaspoon grated lemon
    peel
1 teaspoon grated orange
    peel
2 quarts ginger ale
6 very thin orange slices

Combine spices and 2 cups cider in 1½- or 2-quart glass or enamel saucepan; place over low heat, bring to boiling point, and simmer about 5 minutes. Remove from heat; let stand ½ hour; strain. Combine with remaining cider, grape juice, lemon juice, and lemon and orange peels in large enamel kettle. Pour into glass jars or pitchers to chill.

When ready to serve, pour over ice in punch bowl and add ginger ale. Garnish with orange slices. Makes 35 to 40 punch cup servings.

CHILL AND THRILL

2 cups boiling water
2 teaspoons tea
2 cups light corn syrup or
    1½ cups honey
Salt
¼ teaspoon ground cloves

1 quart loganberry or any
    tart fruit juice
¾ cup lemon juice
2 quarts ginger ale
Fresh mint sprigs
6 thin orange slices
6 whole cloves

228

Add tea to boiling water; cover; steep for 5 minutes. Strain. Combine tea with syrup or honey, few grains salt, and ground cloves in 1½-gallon enamel kettle. Mix and then let cool. Add fruit juice, lemon juice, and ginger ale. Mix and pour over ice in punch bowl. Garnish with fresh mint sprigs. Add orange slices studded with cloves. Makes about 4 quarts, 16 cups, or 24 punch cups.

COLD JUNGLE PUNCH

1 cup sugar	4 cups unsweetened pine-
1½ cups water	apple juice
2 sticks cinnamon	1 cup orange juice
8 whole cloves	½ cup lemon juice

Combine sugar, water, and spices in 2-quart glass or enamel saucepan; place over low heat; boil 3 to 5 minutes. Strain and let cool. Add fruit juices and pour over ice in pitcher or punch bowl. Makes 8 to 10 punch cup servings.

DESERT NIGHT FLOWER

1 quart ginger ale	1 cup orange juice
1 quart water	⅔ cup lemon juice
4 cups unsweetened pine-	½ cup lime juice
apple juice	1 cup sugar
1 cup cranberry juice cocktail	

Chill ginger ale in refrigerator. Put into a large bowl: water, pineapple juice, cranberry juice cocktail, orange juice, lemon juice, and lime juice. Add 1 cup sugar and stir until sugar is dissolved. Chill. When ready to serve, pour mixture into punch bowl. Add the ginger ale and stir to blend. Makes about 3½ quarts. Serves 15.

DR PEPPER PUNCH

1 cup sugar
1 cup water
Juice of 6 lemons, strained
Juice of 6 limes, strained
½ cup grenadine
6 (10 oz.) bottles Dr Pepper

2 quarts chilled soda
2 trays Dr Pepper ice cubes
1 cup maraschino cherries (with stems)

Boil sugar in 1 cup of water over low heat until sugar is completely dissolved. Cool and add to strained juice of lemons and limes, pouring mixture into chilled punch bowl. Stir in grenadine, Dr Pepper, and chilled soda. Add Dr Pepper ice cubes (made by simply pouring Dr Pepper into ice trays, instead of water). Float cherries on the surface or freeze one in each Dr Pepper ice cube.

HUNTER'S PUNCH

1 cup sugar
1 quart water
1 cup strawberry juice
3 lemons, juiced

Juice of 2 oranges
½ can crushed pineapple
1 cup whole strawberries, fresh
1 banana, sliced

230

Combine sugar and water; boil until syrup is formed. Cool. Add strawberry, lemon, and orange juices, and crushed pineapple. Chill thoroughly and let stand for 4 hours. Before serving, mix water and fruit mixture. Then add whole fresh strawberries and sliced banana to punch. Serve with ice.

MOCHA FROST

1 cup heavy cream
½ teaspoon almond
  extract
Few grains of salt

1 quart chilled coffee
1 quart chocolate ice
  cream
¼ teaspoon nutmeg

Whip cream; add extract, and salt. In cold punch bowl, blend coffee and half of ice cream until smooth. Fold in whipped cream and rest of ice cream. Top with nutmeg. Makes 16 punch-cup servings.

PINK PANTHER

4 cans (6-oz. each) rasp-
  berry-lemon punch con-
  centrate, partially
  thawed

1½ quarts club soda,
  chilled
1 lemon, thinly sliced

Combine punch concentrate and club soda in large punch bowl. Add ice. Garnish with lemon slices. Serves 20.

THIRSTY 65

(For large group)

4 cups water
8 cups sugar
7 cups lemon juice
4 cups crushed pineapple,
  not drained
1 cup orange juice
1 cup weak tea

3 gallons water
Crushed ice
Orange slices
Lemon slices
Green and red maraschino
  cherries

231

Boil 4 cups water and 8 cups sugar for 10 minutes and cool. Add lemon juice, pineapple, orange juice and weak tea. Mix and add remaining water. Pour into punch bowl over crushed ice. Make kabobs of an orange slice, a green cherry, a lemon slice, and a red cherry on top threaded on small swizzle sticks or toothpicks. Decorate punch bowl with ivy or garden greens arranged around sides and daisies or gardenias placed in front and back of serving bowl. Dip lemonade into cups or glasses, topping each one with a kabob from the punch bowl. Have an extra supply of kabobs to replenish decoration.

(This lemonade is a little strong to allow for melting ice during time of serving. More water may be added in the beginning if necessary.) Serves about 65.

For God so loved the world, that he gave his only begotten Son, that whosoever believeth in him should not perish, but have everlasting life.
John 3:16

Those who live in the Lord never say goodbye.

232

THE WEDDING PARTY

½ cup sugar
1 cup water
1 can (6 oz.) frozen lemon juice concentrate
1 can (6 oz.) frozen orange-pineapple juice concentrate
1 quart white grape juice

1 jar (6 oz.) maraschino cherries with juice
1 quart ginger ale
Orange slices
1 pint lemon or pineapple sherbet
1 pint lime sherbet
Extra cherries for garnish

Heat sugar and water until sugar is dissolved into a syrup. Cool. Add frozen fruit juice concentrates, grape juice, cherries with juice, and ginger ale to syrup. Mix well and pour into punch bowl. Add ice cubes. Top orange slices with dips of lemon or pineapple and lime sherbet; then top each sherbet dip with a cherry. Add remaining sherbet to punch. Float orange slices with sherbet on surface of punch. Serves about 25.

WEDDING PARTY PUNCH BOWL

30 to 35 mint sprigs
2 cups sugar
2 quarts boiling water
2⅓ cups lemon juice
2 quarts orange juice
1 can (20 oz.) pineapple
  juice

1 quart chilled ginger ale
1 quart chilled sparkling
  water
12 mint sprigs
1 cup thinly slivered
  lemon rind

Wash mint. In 4-quart saucepan, place 30 to 35 mint sprigs, sugar, and water. Simmer, uncovered, 10 minutes. Refrigerate, along with rest of ingredients.

JUST BEFORE SERVING: Strain mint syrup. Add lemon, orange, and pineapple juices; ginger ale; sparkling water. Top with 12 mint sprigs and slivered lemon rind. Serve at once. Serves 50.

Of the gold, the silver, and the brass, and the iron, there is no number. Arise therefore, and be doing, and the Lord be with thee.
1 Chron. 22:16

Procrastination is a tool of the devil—a chain around the arms of progress.

WINDSOR PUNCH

2 sticks cinnamon
12 whole cloves
3 tablespoons loose tea
2 cups boiling water
½ cup sugar
2 cups grape juice

⅓ cup lemon juice
1 teaspoon grated lemon
  rind
1 teaspoon grated orange
  rind
1 quart ginger ale
Block of ice

Combine spices and tea in large pitcher and add boiling water. Brew uncovered about 10 minutes. Stir, strain, and add sugar. Cool at room temperature. Add juices and grated rind. When ready to serve, add ginger ale. Pour over block ice into a punch bowl. Serves 8.

233

DIETER'S DELIGHT

2 cups ice water
⅓ cup nonfat dry milk powder
2 tablespoons strawberry gelatin powder
½ cup fresh, washed, and hulled strawberries (if you are not using a blender, thinly slice strawberries)
Extra strawberries for garnish

Combine all ingredients in a blender or bowl. Beat vigorously until smooth. Pour into chilled glass. Garnish with 2 or 3 fresh strawberries.

Most losers never start the race.

SUNNY DAY

1 cup apple cider
Juice of ½ lemon
3 drops artificial sweetener
¼ teaspoon cinnamon
3 tablespoons water
Mint for garnish

Mix all ingredients and place in refrigerator tray. Freeze to mushy consistency. Remove, place in bowl and beat until smooth. Serve immediately. Garnish with mint.

FOR WEIGHT WATCHERS DRINK AND SMILE

1 cup water
1 tablespoon Sucaryl solution
¼ cup chopped mint leaves
½ cup lemon juice
½ cup unsweetened pineapple tidbits
1 cup orange juice
1 quart orange beverage (artificially sweetened)
Crushed ice
Mint sprigs
Powdered sugar

234

Mix water, sweetener, and mint leaves in a saucepan. Bring to boil; strain and cool. Add lemon juice, pineapple tidbits, and orange juice. Mix well and add orange beverage. Place crushed ice in tall glasses and pour Drink And Smile over ice. Serve with sprig of mint dusted in powdered sugar. Makes 8 servings.

WHEN THE CROWD GATHERS

1 pound coffee, all-purpose
  grind
Cheesecloth bag

6 to 8 quarts water (depending on strength desired)

Wrap coffee in a cheesecloth bag almost twice the size of coffee to allow for expansion. Put boiling water in a large kettle. Let coffee bag down into water, moving up and down several times to be sure of full flavor. Leave coffee in water for about 10 to 15 minutes in a warm place. Before serving time, remove coffee bag and cover kettle to keep coffee hot until serving. Serve as soon as possible. Makes about 35 to 45 cups of coffee.

*A fat purse
does not a good
cook make.*

Proverbs 11:1 A false balance is abomination to the Lord: but a just weight is his delight.

Table of Measurements and Substitution

WEIGHTS AND MEASURES

60 drops . . . . 1 teaspoon
3 teaspoons. . . . . 1 tablespoon
2 tablespoons. . . 1 liquid ounce
4 tablespoons. . . $\frac{1}{4}$ cup
16 tablespoons. . 1 cup
2 cups. . . . . 1 pint
2 pints. . . . . 1 quart
4 quarts . . . . 1 gallon
8 quarts . . . . 1 peck
4 pecks . . . . 1 bushel
16 ounces . . . . . . 1 pound
1 peck potatoes . 15 pounds
1 bushel plums . 50 pounds
1 bushel pears . . 48 pounds
1 bushel
  peaches . . . . . . 48 pounds
1 bushel apples . 44 pounds

COCOA AND CHOCOLATE

For 1 ounce (square) cooking chocolate use 4 tablespoons cocoa and $\frac{1}{2}$ tablespoon fat.
For $\frac{1}{4}$ cup or 4 tablespoons cocoa use 1 ounce (square) chocolate and omit $\frac{1}{2}$ tablespoon fat.

GENERAL EQUIVALENTS

2 cups butter or margarine = 1 pound
1 bouillon cube = 1 teaspoon beef extract
1 tablespoon unflavored gelatin = $\frac{1}{4}$ ounce or $2\frac{2}{3}$ leaves of leaf or French gelatin
Horseradish, 1 tablespoon fresh grated = 2 tablespoons bottled
$1\frac{1}{2}$ cups molasses = 1 cup sugar
1 tablet rennet = 1 tablespoon liquid rennet

MILK

For 1 cup fresh sweet milk in batters use:
  $\frac{1}{2}$ cup evaporated milk and $\frac{1}{2}$ cup water
  1 cup sour milk with $\frac{1}{2}$ teaspoon soda as leavening. Omit 2 teaspoons tartrate or 1 teaspoon double-action baking powder.
  1 cup buttermilk with $\frac{1}{2}$ teaspoon soda as leavening. Omit 2 teaspoons tartrate or 1 teaspoon double-action baking powder.
  1 cup skim milk and 2 tablespoons fat.

FLOUR

For 1 cup sifted enriched flour use any one of the following (sifted if possible) :

1 cup cake flour + 2 table-spoons flour

⅓ cup corn meal + ⅔ cup enriched flour

½ cup corn meal + ½ cup enriched flour

¾ cup bran + ¼ cup enriched flour

½ cup bran + ½ cup enriched flour

½ cup rye flour + ½ cup enriched flour

1 cup rye flour

½ cup whole-wheat flour + ½ cup enriched flour

¾ cup whole-wheat flour + ¼ cup enriched flour

SUGAR

For 1 cup granulated sugar use:

1 cup brown sugar, well packed

¾ cup honey and reduce liquid by 3 tablespoons

1½ cups molasses and reduce liquid by 6 tablespoons

1½ cups sorghum and reduce liquid by 6 tablespoons

2 cups corn syrup and reduce liquid by ½ cup

1½ cups maple syrup and reduce liquid by ½ cup

Vitamins

Vitamins Promote Growth and Protect Health

	Serving		A		B		C	D
	Edible portions as bought	Food as served	Inter-national Units	Thiamine milli-grams	Ribo-flavin milli-grams	Niacin milli-grams	Milli-grams	Inter-National Units
LIVER	3 oz.	2 slices 3″ × 2½″ × ⅜″	17,820	.24	2.45	12.41	15.5	29
HEART	3 oz.	¼ heart 3″ d. × 3½″ lg.	31	.32	.82	5.64	.9	
KIDNEYS	3 oz.	slice 4½″ × 2″ × ½″	705	.21	1.73	6.45	6.2	
BEEF	4 oz.	slice 4½″ × 3″ × ½″	0	.09	.16	5.59	0	
LAMB	4 oz.	slice 4½″ × 3″ × ½″	0	.15	.26	5.93	0	
VEAL	4 oz.	slice 4″ × 2½″ × ½″	0	.14	.31	7.18	0	
PORK	4 oz.	slice 5″ × 3″ × ⅜″	0	.63	.17	3.65	0	
FRANKFURTERS	2 oz.	one 5″ lg. × ¾″ d.	0	.11	.14	1.41		
PORK SAUSAGE	2 oz.	three 3″ lg. × ½″ d.	0	.12	.09	1.31		

238

Food	Amount	Measure						
Poultry	3½ oz.	slice 4″ × 3″ × ½″		.11	.17	6.44	1.8	
Oysters	3½ oz.	5 medium	—	.19	.23	1.25	—	5
Fish	3½ oz.	piece 4″ × 3″ × ½″	570	.04	.07	3.99	1.0	
Eggs	1⅘ oz.	1 egg	300	.04	.13	.02	0	46
Milk	7 oz.	1 glass	312	.07	.34	.22	2.6	4
Butter	⅓ oz.	1 pat	0	—	—	.01	0	4
Bread (Enriched)	2 oz.	2 slices		.14	.09	1.32	0	
Cheese	1 oz.	slice 3″ × 2″ × ¼″	782	.01	.15	.16	0	
Oatmeal	1 oz.	¾ cup	—	.22	.03	.32		
Apples	5 oz.	one 3″ d.	135	.06	.03	.30	6.0	
Oranges	5⅓ oz.	one 2¾ d.	304	.13	.05	.32	80.0	
Bananas	3½ oz.	one 6″ long	430	.09	.06	.60	10.0	
Grapefruit	3½ oz.	one-half 3⅝″ d.	21	.04	.02	.20	40.0	
Prunes	1 oz.	4 medium	482	.03	.05	.51	.9	
Spinach	3½ oz.	½ cup	6,580	.09	.18	.50	32.5	
Potatoes	5 oz.	1 medium	30	.13	.05	1.42	11.3	
Tomatoes	4½ oz.	one 2¾″ d.	1,441	.08	.05	.76	30.1	
Peas	3 oz.	½ cup	468	.23	.12	1.36	12.7	
Carrots	3½ oz.	two 5″ long	10,680	.03	.02	.40	4.6	
Cod Liver Oil	⅙ oz.	1 teaspoon	4,016					104

Food for Thought

To be healthful we must eat a nutritionally balanced ration. This means eating three meals a day, each meal made up of the various types of foods that fulfill body requirements for energy, growth, and repair and that help to induce elimination of waste through the skin, lungs, intestines, and kidneys. The balanced diet will also provide vitamins—those powerful catalysts or agents that work together with minerals to activate the glandular system and release the various elements in food to be utilized as needed.

WHAT PROPORTIONS OF FOOD ELEMENTS ARE NEEDED?

For normal persons, each day's meals should include the number of calories required for the day. Calories are a measure of the amount of energy generated in the body by the three major elements of foods.

PROPORTION OF CALORIES REQUIRED EACH DAY

Proteins . . . . 25 percent
Carbohydrates (sugar and starch) . . . . 55 percent
Fats . . . . 20 percent
Vitamins and Minerals: These are normally present in a balanced diet, which is made up of varied foods so prepared that full nutritive values are retained.

If you study the preceding percentages, you will see that we should eat 5 percent more protein than fat and a little over twice as much carbohydrate as protein.

Protein is digested and utilized by the body more quickly than the other two elements. The carbohydrates are the next to be utilized, and fats come last.

HOW MUCH FOOD OF EACH TYPE MAKES UP A BALANCED DIET?

This can be calculated by planning your meals according to this table worked out by the U.S. Department of Agriculture, and by eating each day the foods it designates. You may eat in addition any foods you want. But the "basic 7" are required in the daily balanced diet.

THE BASIC 7 FOOD GROUPS

Type of Food   **Servings**

Leafy, Green, and Yellow Vegetables .... 1 or more
Citrus Fruit, Tomatoes, Raw Cabbage .... 1 or more
Potatoes and Other Vegetables and Fruits .... 2 or more
Milk, Cheese, Ice Cream .... 3 to 4 cups (children)
                                                                    2 or more (adults)
Meat, Poultry, Fish, Eggs, Dried Peas, Beans .... 1 to 2
Bread, Flour, Cereals
    (whole grain, enriched, or restored) .... every day
Butter and Fortified Margarine .... Some daily

COOKING TO SAVE THE VITAMINS
AND MINERALS IN FOODS

Do not soak vegetables in water before cooking.

Always start food to boil in boiling water, and bring back to boiling point rapidly.

When possible, use short-time methods of cookery in place of long-time methods or cooking processes.

Fry food seldom, as the high temperature necessitated impairs the efficiency of vitamins A, B_1, and C.

Cook vegetables with the skins on when possible, to retain minerals, vitamins, and soluble proteins.

Cover closely all boiling or steaming foods.

Stir foods as little as possible while cooking.

Prepare chopped, diced, or sliced fresh fruits or vegetables just before serving.

Keep foods and all leftover fruit and vegetable juices closely covered in the refrigerator.

Start to cook frozen foods while still frozen.

Use raw frozen foods immediately after thawing.

MEALS FOR LOSING WEIGHT

To reduce at the rate of about 1 pound a week, cut out 500 starch and fat calories from your daily food.

Provide five meals a day—three of them made up of ⅓ protein calories, ⅓ starch and fat calories, and ⅓ bulky fruits and vegetables. The two small "meals" might be a small apple, pear, or orange; or try a cup of black coffee or tea, or peppermint tea with 1 small piece of fruit-flavored candy. Or use bouillon or vegetable broth, vegetable juice, or low-calorie fruit juice. Before retiring, eat a little low-calorie whole fruit or nibble celery or raw carrot.

MEALS FOR GAINING WEIGHT

Eat 500 more calories than usual to gain approximately 1 pound a week.

Provide the usual three balanced square meals a day. In each include 100 extra carbohydrate and fat calories, or add ⅔ of a glass of whole milk. Mid-morning, mid-afternoon, and before retiring, eat 100 or more calories of whatever you like—even cake topped with whipped cream, a double chocolate malted, or an ice cream sundae.

A Note on Seasonings

Make good use of many kinds of herbs and spices for interesting and appetizing seasonings for vegetables and savory foods. This branch of cooking is so important that herbs and spices deserve a small cabinet all to themselves. To the familiar cinnamon, nutmeg, and clove, add curry, chili powder, caraway, basil, poppy or celery seed, and cardamon; garlic and onion salt; herb vinegar; mixed herbs, thyme, marjoram, flaked parsley, and mint; sage, poultry seasoning, and many others. If you buy them one at a time, you'll never miss the money. Use as indicated in this book. You'll be thrilled with the chic new flavors of your foods.

HOW TO USE HERBS

Herbs may be used fresh, dried, or powdered.

1 tablespoon any minced fresh herb = 1 teaspoon of a dried herb or ¼ teaspoon powered herb.

Always reconstitute a dried herb by steeping it 5 minutes in barely enough hot liquid to cover —water or stock for soups and most sauces; milk for a cream sauce; lemon or fresh lime juice for salads. Add the liquid with the herb.

To KEEP FRESH HERBS: Rinse in cold water, dry on paper towels, place in a glass jar and cover (or wrap in aluminum foil) and refrigerate. They will keep fresh for several days.

To MINCE FRESH HERBS: Use kitchen scissors.

PREPARED SEASONINGS

Certain prepared seasonings lift up certain foods, but in using them one must be careful not to over-season or under-season, but rather to obtain a delicious blend that will bring out the flavor of the predominant ingredient in the dish.

MONOSODIUM GLUTAMATE: Known as MSG, it is an important seasoning for all savory foods. It is derived from vegetable proteins and has the property of magnifying natural flavors. It is used by good chefs all over the world. Several brands are on the market; the most widely distributed is called "Accent." Use from ½ to 1 teaspoon to the pound before cooking meat, poultry, or fish, and ½ teaspoon to the pound after cooking vegetables. Add ¼ teaspoon when cooking any savory sauce.

FINES HERBES: A mixture of delicately flavored herbs such as parsley, chervil, savory, and burnet. Always added at the end of the cooking.

STRONG HERBS: Such as sage, basil, mint, dill, rosemary, thyme, and marjoram. Always added during the cooking.

BOUQUET GARNI: A spray of parsley, stalk of celery, sprig of thyme, and sometimes a leek and a bay leaf—tied together. Cook in soup or when boiling fish to season it.

KETCHUP, CHILI SAUCE, TABLE MUSTARD, AND HORSERADISH: All lend themselves to fish and meat dishes; to mayonnaise and boiled salad dressings; and to white sauce for cauliflower, celery, nut loaves, etc.

PICKLES, RIPE AND GREEN OLIVES, CHOW-CHOW, CHUTNEYS, AND THE LIKE: Use especially with fish and fat meats like ham; pot roast; and baked beans. They may be added to vegetable, nut, and cheese salads. Olives are good with poultry.

WORCESTERSHIRE POWDER, MEAT SAUCE, AND TABASCO: Should be used to accent meat, fish, sauces, and bland foods such as eggs or tossed salads.

Index

247

249

French Loaf with Parsley Butter, 179
French Quarter Pralines, 205
French Style Peas, 149
Fresh Buttered Carrots, 137
Fresh Peach Broil, 201
Fricassee of Liver Francoise, 95
Frijoles, 81
Fritter Corn Bread, 180
Frosted Coffee, 217
Fruit:
  Apple Cream Pie, 188
  Apricot Meringue Torte, 196
  Arctic Fruit Salad, 49
  Bananas Mediterranean, 197
  Broiled Grapefruit Northern, 199
Carrot Salad Hawaiian, 55
  Cherry Cobbler Jubilee, 188
  Cherry Meringues, 197
  Coconut Soup Polynesian, 43
Cottage Cheese-Cranberry Salad, 50
  Crepes d'Orange with Orange Hard Sauce 199, 200
  Emerald Mound Salad, 47
Fresh Peach Broil, 201
Fruit Cocktail Orange Jello, 207
  Fruit Coconut Dessert in Melon Halves, 198
  Grapefruit Pie, 189
  Holiday Fruit Soup, 42
  Hot Applesauce Compote, 207
  Lemon-Coconut Icing, 193
  Miami Beach Lime Chiffon Dessert, 206
  Miami Fruit Salad Platter with Citrus Dressing, 48
  Miniature Apple Dumplings, 187
  Orange-Nut Frozen Sundae, 200
  Peach Catsup Garnish, 35

Peach Melba—Melba Sauce, 202
Peach Waffle Shortcake, Boston, 201
Pineapple Upside-down Cake, 192
Raspberry Cheese Bouquet, 50
Strawberry Long Cake, 194
Swiss Strawberry Cheese Cake, 195

G

Galveston Fried Oysters, 111
Garden Fresh Kabobs, 30
Garden Pasta, 163
German Mocha, 215
Ginger Fizz, 221
Gingerbread Cutouts, 192
Gourmet Salad with French Dressing, 58
Grapefruit Pie, 189
Grape Hawaiian Punch, 221
Green Beans:
  Barbecued Wax Beans, 129
  Cashew Green Beans, 124
  Celery-French Green Bean Medley, 122
  Green Beans and Onions, Tempura, 123
  Green Beans Carolina, 122
  Green Bean Pickles, Vermont, 36
  Spicy Green Beans, 124
  Yankee Doodle Bean Ring, 123
Green Peas and Green Limas, Roma, 167
Guacamole Salad, 51
Gulfstream Shrimp Snacks, 31

H

Ham:
  Broiled Ham Slices, 87

W

Y